A Book of Angels

D0956218

Other books by Marigold Hunt
from Sophia Institute Press®:

The First Christians

Schooled by St. Patrick

A Life of Our Lord for Children

Marigold Hunt

A Book of Angels

Stories of Angels in the Bible

SOPHIA INSTITUTE PRESS®
Manchester, New Hampshire

A *Book of Angels* was originally published in 1958 by Sheed and Ward, New York. This 2004 edition by Sophia Institute Press® contains minor editorial revisions to the original text.

Copyright © 2004 Sophia Institute Press®

Printed in the United States of America

All rights reserved

Illustrations and cover design by Theodore Schluenderfritz

No part of this book may be reproduced, stored in a retrieval system, or transmitted in any form, or by any means, electronic, mechanical, photocopying, or otherwise, without the prior written permission of the publisher, except by a reviewer, who may quote brief passages in a review.

Sophia Institute Press®
Box 5284, Manchester, NH 03108
1-800-888-9344
www.sophiainstitute.com

Nihil obstat: John A. Goodwin, J.C.D., *Censor Librorum*
Imprimatur: Francis Cardinal Spelling, Archbishop of New York

Library of Congress Cataloging-in-Publication Data

Hunt, Marigold.
    A book of angels : stories of angels in the Bible / Marigold Hunt.—
[Rev. ed.].
        p. cm.
    ISBN 1-933184-00-0 (pbk. : alk. paper)
    1. Angels — Juvenile literature. I. Title.

BT966.H78 2004
235'.3 — dc22   2004024706

04 05 06 07 08 09 10 9 8 7 6 5 4 3 2 1

Contents

A Book of Angels

Chapter One

About Angels and Devils and Us

The one thing everybody knows about angels is that we can't see them. Of course it's true that we can't, but it isn't the most interesting thing about angels. You can't see the wind either, but there is plenty you can know about it besides that.

The reason you can't see angels is interesting to start with. What can you see of your own self? You can see your hands and feet and quite a lot of your body, and if you look into a mirror, you can see your face. But there is more to you than that. You have a mind to know with and a will to choose and love with. Have you ever seen them? No, of course not, nor has anyone else. And the reason you can't see an angel is that he is *all* mind and will. He has no body, so he doesn't show at all. God is all mind and will, too, which is why you can't see Him either.

That is what people mean when they say God is a spirit and the angels are spirits and our souls are spirits. Only spirits have minds for knowing with and wills for loving with.

A Book of Angels

God, just as it says in the catechism, is the Supreme Spirit. His mind is so great that no one else will ever altogether understand it. And His will is so strong that He can do anything at all and love more than we can ever understand. The first people He made were angels. They are more like Him than anything else He made: very strong and wonderful mind-and-will people. He made them to know Him and love Him and be happy with Him forever.

Of course, God made this world we live in, too. He made all the things we *can* see: the sun and the sea and the mountains, flowers and animals and birds. But He didn't make them to last forever.

Some of them last quite a long time. The sun has been shining for millions of years and will probably shine for a million more. Mountains go on looking much the same for hundreds of years, and so does the sea. Some things last only a very little while; butterflies and flowers are of this sort. But nothing of all the things we can see is made to last forever. That is the really tremendous difference between angels and this world. Each angel was made to last forever, and this world is not. Only spirits are made to last forever.

What about us? We are mind-and-will people, just as the angels are. Our souls are spirits made to last forever. But we have bodies, too, and they belong to this world and come to an end. We are the only things God made that belong half to the world of the angels and half to this world we can see. Our bodies are just as much part of us as

4

our souls, and God has made a special arrangement about them. No matter when we die, at the end of the world we shall have our own bodies back again. They will be so wonderfully made over for us that they will last as long as our souls do. And that will be forever and ever and ever.

In the meantime, here we are among all the wonderful and interesting things that God made and that we can see. It's rather easy for us to forget all about the things we can't see, but it's a great pity if we do. We shall never get to Heaven if we are not even interested in it! And God has given each of us an angel especially to look after us and to help us get there.

This is a book of stories about angels from the Bible. And the first thing someone will say is, "You said we couldn't see angels, but all these stories are about angels people *did* see!"

And that's quite true. When God sends an angel with a message for us, and wants us to see him, of course he must appear somehow. Even then what we see isn't really the angel himself. It's just a body God gives him for the occasion, so that he can let us know he's there. It isn't the angel's body; it is more as if he brought along a picture and held it up for us to see, so that we would know he had come.

All the same, we can learn a good deal about angels by finding out what has been said about them by the people they have appeared to. They do not usually try to describe what they saw. When they do try, you can see how difficult they find it to explain how the angel looked. Ezekiel and Isaiah, whose stories are in this book, both describe visions of angels, and you'll see how difficult they found it, and how hard it is to make a picture in your mind of just what they saw. Sometimes, if it suits God's plan, an angel appears who looks just like a man, so that no one knows the difference. But artists usually draw them with wings, so that we can tell which of the people in a picture are angels.

Suppose God sent an angel to see you and wanted you to know he was an angel. What would he look like? He would probably look enough like pictures of angels you have seen for you to guess that that was what he was. But he would look a great deal grander and more wonderful than any picture you ever saw, because angels are so much more wonderful than any picture an artist can make.

Sometimes you see pictures and stories of angels that show them as babies or small children with tiny wings, sitting on little clouds. These stories and pictures are not really meant to show what angels are like; stories of baby angels are fairy tales. There is no such thing as a baby angel. From the first moment that God made them, the angels have been just as they are now and just as they always will be.

Because all the stories in this book come from the Bible, you may be sure that all of them are very well worth reading. God would never have let them get into the Bible if they were not.

The very first angel in the Bible is the Devil! The Devil is a wicked angel, of course. Wonderful as the good angels are, God did not allow them to begin being happy with Him forever in Heaven until they had been given some kind of trial. God wanted them to choose whether or not they would love Him and serve Him.

We don't know what sort of trial would suit an angel, but we do know that some of them failed in the one God gave them. One great angel refused to love and serve God; he wanted to be served and worshiped himself, as if *he* were God!

"I will not serve!" he said, and some of the other angels said the same. Then there was a great battle between the good angels and the bad angels.

The good angels were led by Michael, whose name means "Who is like God?" That was the very first battle in a war that has gone on ever since between the good angels and the bad angels. That first battle ended in the bad angels' being cast out of Heaven forever. That's why we say, "Holy Michael the Archangel, defend us on the day of battle."

The bad angels were given no chance to be sorry. Do you know why God gives us so many chances to be sorry and gave the bad angels no second chance at all? It is

7

because a second chance wouldn't be of any use to an angel. Once angels make up their minds, they never change them. That is because whatever an angel wants to understand, he does understand, straight off, as well as he ever can. If an angel wanted to study arithmetic, he would only have to turn his mind toward it, and he would understand the whole thing. He wouldn't have to bother about remembering how many sevens make eighty-four or even working out one sum.

We learn things slowly, bit by bit, and forget many things, too. We are always changing our minds and being sorry, because every time we learn something new or remember something, we see things differently. But when the bad angels chose to refuse to love and obey God, they knew exactly what they were doing. They will never understand it more clearly than they did at the first moment; they will never see anything new to make them think differently. There was nothing to do but send them away forever.

The devils are still spirits, and they must continue to be spirits forever because spirit is made to last forever. They are great spirits who hate God instead of loving Him, and oh, how they hate us, too! We have the chance of going to Heaven and being happy there with God and with the good angels forever — the chance the bad angels threw away. So they will do anything to keep us from getting there.

Chapter Two

The Beginning of Everything

The Bible begins with the story of God making the world and the sky and everything in them, from stars to grass and fishes. He made everything, and everything He made was good. Last of all, God made us.

This is the story of the first man and woman and of the first angel in the Bible — a bad angel.

It was from the clay of the ground that the Lord God made man, and He breathed into him the breath of life, so that he became a living person. God had planted a garden for this man to live in. Here grew all the trees that are most delightful to look at and that have the best fruit. The man was to look after the garden and tend the trees. In the middle of it grew the Tree of Life and the tree that gives knowledge of good and evil.

God gave the man this command: "You may eat as much as you like of the fruit of every tree in the garden, except the fruit of the Tree of Knowledge of Good and Evil. If you eat that, you will die."

And now God said, "This man needs a companion. I must make a wife for him."

But first God brought all the animals and birds to Adam to see what he would call them. Adam gave them all names, and the names he gave them are their names still. But there was no animal among them all who was of the same kind as Adam.

Then God sent Adam into a deep sleep, and while he slept, God took one of Adam's ribs and made it into a woman. When God brought the woman to Adam, he was delighted.

"She shall be called woman," he said, "this which you have taken from me."

Adam and his wife had never worn clothes, nor felt any need to. They went naked and were not ashamed.

Adam called his wife *Eve*, "life," because she was to be the mother of all the people who were ever to live in this world.

Of all the animals God had made, none was so cunning as the snake. It was the snake who said to the woman, "Why has God told you not to eat the fruit of any of the trees in this garden?"

"We do eat the fruit of the trees in this garden," said Eve, "all except one. That is the Tree of the Knowledge of Good and Evil. God has told us we must not touch that, or we shall die."

"Nonsense!" said the snake. "You will not die. God knows very well that as soon as you eat the fruit of that tree, your eyes will be opened and you will be like God, knowing good and evil as He does."

Eve went to look at the tree. The fruit was beautiful and looked as if it would be very good to eat. She picked some and ate it; and it tasted good. So she picked some more and took it to Adam, and they ate it together.

And what happened? Something was changed; they didn't know what it was, but they did know they felt suddenly ashamed of being naked. And for the first time they felt afraid of God.

They tried to make themselves clothes from the big leaves of a fig tree.

And presently they heard the voice of God as He walked in the garden in the cool of the evening. They hid from God among the trees. And they heard Him call, "Adam, where are you?"

"I heard Your voice," said Adam, "and I was afraid because I am naked, so I hid myself."

"What is this about nakedness?" said God. "Have you been eating the fruit of the tree I forbade you to touch?"

"The woman You gave me for a companion brought me fruit," said Adam. "That is how I came to eat it."

Then the Lord God said to the woman, "What made you do this?"

"It was the snake," said Eve. "He lied to me and deceived me, and I ate the fruit."

Then the Lord God spoke to the snake, "For doing this," He said, "you shall crawl on your belly; all your life you shall crawl and you shall eat dust. And I will make war between you and the woman, between your children and her Child. He will crush your head when you are lying in wait to bite His heel."

To Eve, God said, "You have let pain into the world, and you will have to suffer it. And you will be under your husband's power."

To Adam, He said, "You listened to your wife's advice and ate the fruit that I forbade you to eat. And now, through what you have done, the earth is under a curse. All your life you shall get your food from it by hard work; it will grow thorns and thistles more easily than anything you plant. You will always have to toil for your food until you go back to the ground from which you were taken. You were made from dust, and to the dust you must return."

And He made Adam and Eve clothes from the skins of animals, and He said, "Now Adam has become like one of us, knowing good and evil! He cannot be allowed to eat from the Tree of Life and live endlessly."

So God banished Adam and Eve from the garden He had made for them. He sent them out into the world to get their living as best they could. And He set an angel with a sword of flame at the gate of the garden, so that they could never return or reach the Tree of Life again.

This is a wonderful story, and it has a sad ending. Did the man who wrote it down mean for us to suppose that everything happened just as he said, as if he were a newspaper reporter, writing an account of what he had seen? Everything in the story happened thousands and thousands and thousands of years before he was born, so it doesn't seem very likely. No, he was telling a story he knew, about the way God made the world and about the first people He made. He told it just as God wanted it told, and he told it to teach us four very important things. First, that God did make the world and everything else there is.

He didn't really know just how long God took to do it, or how He did it. But he knew God made everything, and that is the first important thing to know. The second is that everything God made is good.

And the third is that God made us to live forever: first in this world, and then in Heaven, and with no death in between, even for our bodies. And the fourth is that the very first pair of people He made spoiled the whole plan by choosing to do what the Devil told them instead of what God told them.

Why not just write down those four things? Because God wanted them to be told as part of a story; people remember stories better than anything else. That's why our Lord told so many stories when He came to teach us.

The snake in the story is the Devil, of course, although the story doesn't say so. But bad angels, as well as good ones, usually show us something of what they are like when they appear to us, so the writer chose a snake to be the Devil's disguise. A snake is rather a good picture of the Devil: a slithery, sneaky thing that hides and gives you a poisonous bite when you are not expecting it.

The Tree of Life in the story is a symbol, and a lovely one, too. A symbol is something that stands for something else. It sounds difficult, but it isn't really. We all use symbols all the time without even noticing we are doing it. There is a statue of a lady with a torch in New York Harbor called the Statue of Liberty. Everybody knows what it means, and nobody supposes that Liberty is really a lady with a torch. She stands for an idea that you couldn't possibly make a statue of. In just the same way, a picture of the Sacred Heart stands for our Lord's love for us, and in many holy pictures, a dove stands for the Holy Spirit.

What is the Tree of Life a symbol of? It is symbol of the gift of life everlasting that God gave to Adam and Eve and meant for all mankind. The same symbol has been used in many pictures and is used again at the end of the Bible, as you will see.

What about the Tree of the Knowledge of Good and Evil? So far, Adam and Eve knew only good things. Everything in the whole world God had made was good and beautiful and happy, and so were they. The Devil was evil, of course, but he had no place in God's wonderful new world, and no power there, unless they gave it to him. The only way they could learn evil was by bringing it into the world by sin, and that is just what they did, and it was the Devil who persuaded them to do it. So they learned evil and learned something new about good, too: how terrible it is to lose it.

Just what they did, whether it was eating forbidden fruit, like Adam and Eve, or something quite different, we don't know. But we know why they did it. What tempted them was the Devil's promise: "You shall be like gods, knowing good and evil."

The Devil meant really that instead of taking God's word for it, they should set themselves up as judges of what is good and what is bad. It was as if they said to God, "We don't need You to tell us what's good for us; we know just as much about it as You do. What we say is good for us is good, and what we say is bad is bad." They wanted to be able to make things good or evil as they chose, not just to know about them. They were being proud and disobedient, and most terribly ungrateful. And pretty silly, too. In fact, they were behaving remarkably like the bad angels — and no wonder, as it was one of those angels who gave them the idea.

Their sin was the first sin committed by men, and surely the worst sin. And all because they wanted to be like gods!

The odd thing is that God had already made them more like Him than they needed to be to be happy. He didn't just mean them to be as happy as they could imagine being forever. No, He meant them to be as happy as He wanted them to be forever. And that is a thousand, thousand times happier. He had given them a share of His own life in their souls that would make them able to live with Him in Heaven.

That is the greatest gift of all, and it was given to them free, on top of everything else.

Even the angels could not live in Heaven without this gift; it was given to them, too. The good angels kept it; the bad angels lost it. When Adam and Eve obeyed the bad angel, they lost it also, of course. They shut the doors of Heaven in their own faces — and the doors stayed shut. We are all born without that share of God's life in our souls. That is why we need to be baptized.

Besides losing that great gift, Adam and Eve had let pain and death into the world and spoiled everything. Life was meant to be so easy and pleasant for us, but since then, it has always been hard and difficult.

If someone starts a forest fire, he may be very sorry afterward, but he won't be able to undo what he has done. All the living things in the forest — birds and beasts and flowers, as well as trees — are gone. There is nothing left but burnt ground and blackened tree stumps. Everything is spoiled. All the sorrow in the world will not make the forest as it was before the fire.

It was like that with Adam and Eve's sin. They were sorry, and God forgave them. But they had let evil into the world and spoiled it, and what they had done they could not undo. No more could any of the men who came after them. Nothing would ever again be quite as it had been before their sin.

But if men were helpless, God was not. He had a great plan for the world, a wonderful plan. He meant to make everything even better than it had been to begin with. No one but God was to know of His plan for thousands and thousands of years. But so that Adam and Eve should not feel too hopeless, He gave a hint at once that the Devil would not be allowed to have his way with the world forever.

He gave this hint when He said to the Devil, "I will make war between you and the woman, and between your children and her Child. He will crush your head when you are lying in wait to bite His heel." God did not tell them what it meant: that one day He would come into the spoiled world Himself, become a man, and die to redeem us. But when the right time came, many thousands of years later, He began to prepare the world for His coming.

The Old Testament tells how God prepared the world for His coming, and the New Testament tells what happened when He came. The Old Testament begins with this story about a bad angel, and the New Testament ends in a perfect blaze of good angels.

In between there are all kinds of angels, good and bad, more than you will find in this book. But there are enough stories of angels here to give you an idea of how busy God keeps the good angels in helping us to get to Heaven, and how desperately the bad ones try to get us to go to their home in Hell.

Chapter Three

Abraham, Isaac, and Jacob

Abraham came from a city called Ur in Chaldea — a country southeast of Palestine. He was chosen by God to be the first of a whole nation of people who were to learn about the true God and how they ought to worship Him. They were to be God's Chosen People, and all were descended from one man, Abraham. God had chosen a country for them to live in, Canaan, which we call Palestine. All this was the beginning of God's great plan to come Himself and save us. God could have chosen any man in the whole world to be the first of His Chosen People, and He chose Abraham. This makes Abraham a very special person.

This is how it all began:

The Lord said to Abraham, "Leave your country behind and your own people, and come to a land I will show you. There I will make you the father of a whole nation. I will bless you and make your name famous, and in you all the peoples of the world shall find a blessing."

So Abraham set out as God had told him to. He took his wife, Sara, with him and his nephew Lot. These three, with all their servants and possessions, set out for the Land of Canaan. There were people living there then called Canaanites, and it was their country. But when Abraham reached it, God appeared to him and promised that He would give the whole country to Abraham's descendants.

In Canaan, Abraham grew rich, and so did his nephew Lot. They each had flocks of sheep and goats and herds of cattle, and camels. They camped in Canaan wherever there was good grass for all these animals to eat, and water for them to drink. When the grass in one place was all eaten, Abraham and Lot moved their camps to a new place. The Canaanites did not bother much about them as a rule, because these people lived mostly down in the plains, and Abraham and Lot up in the hilly part of the country.

Abraham and Lot had to move camp often; so many animals ate all the grass very fast. The richer they grew, the bigger the herds of animals were, and the more people were needed to look after them. They had dairymaids and shepherds and camel drivers and men to guard all these, and most of them were married, with families, so that altogether they were a great company. In fact, there were too many people. When Abraham's shepherds began to quarrel with Lot's shepherds about the well they were using, Abraham saw what must be done.

He said to Lot, "We cannot have this quarreling between our people. We all ought to be good friends, and I

can see there will be no peace until we part from one another. See, the whole land lies before you. Choose which
way you will go, and I will go in the other direction."
They were high up in the hills and could see a long way.

Lot looked about him and saw the deep valley through
which the river Jordan flows to the Dead Sea, and the
plain at the head of the Dead Sea. From where they were
standing, the country below looked like a rich and lovely
garden. So Lot chose to go that way, and Abraham went
back into the hills. Down on the plain stood two cities,
Sodom and Gomorrah, and after a time Lot settled in
Sodom.

When Lot and all his herds and people had gone, God
spoke to Abraham again. "Look about you," God said.
"Look to the north and south and east and west. All the
land you can see I give to you and to your descendants after you. I will make your descendants a whole nation;
there will be so many of them that they will be as impossible to count as the grains of sand."

Abraham was grateful, but he was puzzled, too. He
and Sara had no children, and they were getting old.
How could he have all these descendants if he had not
even one child of his own? So when, in another vision,
God said to him, "Have no fear. I am here to protect you,
and I mean to give you a great reward," Abraham said,
"What do You mean to give me, Lord? I have no son. A
slave, the son of one of my servants, will inherit all I
have."

"He will not be your heir," said God. "You shall have a son of your own. Look up at the sky, and see if you can count the stars. Your descendants, like the stars, will be too many to count."

Abraham put his faith in God. But he and Sara still had no child. In those days, it was quite ordinary for men to have more than one wife. So Sara said to Abraham, "God has given me no children, and I am getting old. Marry my maidservant Agar as a second wife. If she has children, it will at least be better than no children at all."

So Abraham married Agar. And Agar did have a baby, a boy, and they called him Ishmael.

⁀

Some time after this, when Abraham was camped in the valley of Mambre, he was sitting one day in the shade by the tent door. It was noon and a hot day. Presently he looked up and saw three men who seemed to be travelers standing a little way off.

Abraham ran to meet them and bowed politely. "Lord," he said to the one who seemed to be the leader of the three, "do not pass your servant by. Come and rest in the shade by my tent, and I will bring you water to wash your feet, something to eat and drink, too; you must be refreshed before you continue on your journey."

The three sat down in the shade gratefully and Abraham hurried into his tent to find Sara. "Quick," he said to her, "make some griddle cakes. We have visitors."

Then he ran to the byre and chose a calf, which he ordered to be killed and cooked. When it was ready, he brought out Sara's griddle cakes, butter and milk and broiled veal and set a meal for the three visitors. He stood beside them in the shade of the trees as they ate.

When they had finished, one of them said, "Where is your wife, Sara?"

"She is here, in the tent," said Abraham.

"When I come back, this time next year," said the visitor, "Sara will have a son."

Sara could hear them speaking from where she was in the tent. And when she heard that, she laughed to herself. "What!" she thought, "me to have a baby at my age!"

She supposed the visitor was just being polite and had no idea she was an old woman. But the visitor said to Abraham, "Why does Sara laugh and ask whether she is really to be a mother in her old age? Is anything too difficult for God? At this time next year, I shall come this way again, as I said, and Sara will have a son of her own."

Sara came tumbling out of the tent, very frightened. "I did not laugh!" she said.

"Ah!" said the visitor, "but you did laugh!"

Sara didn't mean to tell a lie; she was too frightened to think.

When the visitors got up to go on with their journey, Abraham went with them to set them on their way, which was toward Sodom. He had beautiful manners and had been polite and kind to them, just because they were strangers and on a journey. But now it seemed to him that these were no ordinary travelers. Two he guessed to be angels and the third God Himself. And he was quite right.

The one he had guessed to be God said as they walked along, "Why should I hide what I mean to do from Abraham, this man who is to be the father of a great nation? This man through whom all the nations of the world are to be blessed? Have I not chosen him as one who will teach his children and all who come after him to follow the ways which the Lord shows them and to do what is right?"

Then He turned to Abraham and said, "I have heard terrible things of Sodom and Gomorrah. Their wickedness is beyond believing. I am going to see for myself if all I have heard of them is true; I must know for certain. If all I have heard is true, they must be destroyed."

The two angels were walking on ahead toward Sodom, and Abraham was alone with God. He came close to Him and said, "Will You then sweep away innocent men along with the guilty ones? Suppose there are fifty innocent men in Sodom: must they die because the rest are wicked? Surely it would not be like You to destroy the good with the guilty?"

Abraham was worried about Sodom; his nephew Lot lived there.

"If I find fifty good men in Sodom," said the Lord, "I will spare the whole city."

"What if there should be five less than fifty?" said Abraham. "Will You lay the whole city in ruins for lack of five good men?"

"No," said the Lord. "If there are forty-five good men there, the city will not be destroyed."

"What if there should be forty?" said Abraham.

"I will not strike the city if there are forty good men," said the Lord.

"Do not be angry with me, Lord," said Abraham. "But what if there are thirty?"

"If I find thirty," said the Lord, "I will not do it."

"What if there are twenty?" said Abraham.

"They shall all live," said the Lord, "if twenty deserve to."

"And suppose there are just ten?" said Abraham.

"I will even spare the city from destruction," said the Lord, "to save ten." So God finished speaking to Abraham and went on toward Sodom.

Abraham looked out over the plain from where he had been speaking to the Lord. He could see the cities down there in the distance; he stood looking at them for a few minutes, and then he went home.

☞

It was evening when the two angels reached Sodom. Lot was sitting by the gates of the town. When he saw them, he stood up and bowed to them as his uncle, Abraham, had done, and invited them to have supper and spend the night at his house.

That night, after they had had supper, the angels said to Lot: "Is there anyone else here, any relation of yours, besides your wife and your two daughters? If so, find them. They must leave this city without delay. We have been sent by the Lord to destroy it for its wickedness, which He Himself has seen."

Lot was amazed when he heard this. He had no other relations there, but his daughters were both engaged to be married, so he went out to find the men they were engaged to. He found them, but they would not listen to him. They thought his talk about the city being destroyed was some kind of joke. So Lot had to come home without them. He was very slow about getting ready to leave; perhaps he wasn't too sure himself that what the angels said was really going to happen. At last the angels had to hustle him and his family out of the town. They led them outside the city and said, "Now fly for your lives! Do not stop for anything until you reach the hills, and do not look behind you, or you will be killed."

Lot and his wife and daughters ran. But his wife could not resist stopping to look behind her to see what was happening, and as she stood there, she turned into a pillar of salt.

That morning, Abraham was up early. He walked out to the place where he had stood talking to God the day before, and looked over the plain. But now there were no cities to be seen there, only smoke rising and drifting from where they had been.

Next year, just as God had foretold, Sara had a son. She and Abraham gave him the name Isaac, because that sounds like the word for *laughter* in their language, and Sara had laughed when she first heard she was to have a baby.

When Isaac was about a year old, Sara saw Agar's son, Ishmael, teasing her baby. Sara was furious. She went to Abraham and said, "Send that slave woman and her son away. I will not have Ishmael sharing everything with my son, Isaac."

Abraham did not want to do this at all. It seemed most unfair, and besides, he was very fond of Ishmael.

But God said to him, "Do what Sara wants you to, and do not worry about it. It is through your son Isaac that my promises to you will be fulfilled. But I will make Ishmael the first of a great nation, too, because he is also your son."

So next morning, Abraham brought a bottle of water and some food to Agar and told her she must take her son and go.

Poor Agar had no idea where to go. She wandered about in the desert with little Ishmael. At last, all the water in the bottle was drunk, and she could find no well anywhere. She and Ishmael were both beginning to be very thirsty. At last she gave up in despair, put Ishmael down under a bush, and went and sat a little way off. "I cannot bear to see my son die," she said, and she cried bitterly.

Ishmael was crying, too, and God had heard him. His angel called to Agar from Heaven, "What is the matter, Agar? Do not be afraid. Get up, and take the child by the hand. I mean to make him the founder of a great nation."

God showed Agar where there was a well of water; she could have seen it before if she had not been crying so hard! She filled the water bottle and gave Ishmael a drink, and everything began to get better.

Ishmael did grow up safely, and he became a great archer. The nation descended from him are those people called Arabs.

⌐

It was some time after this that God put Abraham's faith to a last great test. Abraham had believed God's word when God told him he would be the father of a great nation, even though he had no son. And he believed God again when He said that Sara would have a son in her old age. He had sent Agar and his eldest son away because God told him to; now he had only Isaac. This is what happened:

"Abraham, Abraham!" called God from Heaven.

"I am here at Your command," said Abraham.

"Take your beloved son Isaac," said the voice of God, "and go to the land of Clear Vision. There you are to kill your son and offer him to me as a burnt sacrifice. I will show you the mountain where it is to be done."

Poor Abraham! He really thought God meant it. To the people of other religions who lived around him, it was quite an ordinary thing to kill one of their children as a sacrifice to their horrible make-believe gods. Abraham did not know God well enough yet to realize how different He was from them. It looked to Abraham like the end of all his hopes, but he still trusted God. If God said he must do this, he must, however miserable it made him, and however much it seemed to make nonsense of all God's promises to him.

So at dawn the next day, Abraham cut the wood needed for the fire for a burnt sacrifice and saddled his ass. Then he told two of his menservants to follow him and set off with Isaac for the land of Clear Vision.

After they had traveled for two days, Abraham saw the mountain God had told him about. No one is quite certain, but it was most likely Mount Moriah, where one day God's Temple was to stand.

"Wait here with the ass," said Abraham to his two servants. "I and my son are going up this mountain to offer worship to God. Wait for us here."

Abraham gave the wood to Isaac to carry, and he himself took fire in a brazier and a knife.

As they walked along together, Isaac said, "Father."

"What is it, my son?" said Abraham.

"We have the fire and the wood for the sacrifice," said Isaac, "but where is the lamb we are to offer?"

"My son," said poor Abraham, "God will give us a lamb to be sacrificed."

They went on together until they reached the place God had shown Abraham. Here he built an altar of stones and laid the wood on it. Then he bound Isaac and laid him on top of the wood. And he reached out and took hold of the knife to kill his son.

But an angel of the Lord called to him from Heaven, "Abraham! Abraham!"

When he answered, "Here I am, at your command," the angel said, "Do not hurt the boy. I know now that you fear God; for His sake you were ready to give up even your only son."

And Abraham, looking about, saw a ram caught by its horns in some bushes. He took that and killed it and offered it to God as a burnt sacrifice, instead of his son. Before he left the place, the angel called to him again from Heaven: "This is the message the Lord has for you," he said. "I have sworn by my own Name to reward you for what you did; you were ready to give up your only son for my sake. More and more will I bless you, more and more will I increase the people to be descended from you. They shall indeed be as uncountable as the stars in the sky or the grains of sand by the seashore. Your descendants shall conquer all their enemies; all the races of the world shall find a blessing in them because you were ready to do what I asked of you."

Then Abraham and Isaac went back to where the servants waited with the ass, and so returned home again.

And never after that did Abraham, or any of those who came after him, suppose that God could really want a child killed in sacrifice to Him.

When Isaac grew up and married, he had twin sons. Their names were Jacob and Esau, and they did not get along well with each other. Esau married two wives. Both of them were Canaanite girls. The Canaanites were the people among whom Abraham and his family lived. They were all right in their way, no doubt, but they worshiped idols. Isaac and his wife Rebecca couldn't bear them.

Isaac told Jacob not to marry a Canaanite, but to go and find a wife for himself among his own people. Jacob set off at once to visit his uncle, Laban, who lived far away in Mesopotamia. He hoped one of his daughters might marry him. Nowadays we do not like first cousins to marry each other, but in those days, it was thought to be all right.

It was while he was on his way to his uncle's house that Jacob saw angels. He was walking toward a town called Haran, but it began to get dark while he was still some distance from it, out in the country. Jacob decided to spend the night where he was. It was quite warm, so he just lay down on the ground with his head on a stone for a pillow, and went to sleep.

In his sleep, Jacob dreamed that he saw a ladder stretching from earth up to Heaven, and the angels were using it as a stairway. He lay watching them, and presently he saw God Himself lean down over the top of the ladder. God spoke to him, giving him again the same promise He had given to his grandfather Abraham. "I am the Lord," He said. "The God of your father, Isaac, and of your grandfather Abraham. The ground you are lying on is my gift to you and to your children after you. Your descendants shall be as hard to count as the grains of dust. They shall overflow their country on every side, and all the people of the earth shall find a blessing in you and in these descendants of yours. I myself will watch over you wherever you go, and I will bring you back to this land again. All my promises to you will be fulfilled."

When Jacob woke up, he said, "This is the Lord's dwelling place, the very gate of Heaven. And I slept here and never knew it!" He set up the stone he had used as a pillow to mark the place and called it *Bethel*, which means "the House of God."

Jacob went on with his journey. He married one of Laban's daughters called Leah and afterward another one called Rachel. And he married more wives after that. Altogether he had twelve sons. He stayed a long time with his uncle Laban, but at last they all went home to Canaan.

Abraham, Isaac, and Jacob

It was God Himself who gave Jacob a new name: Israel. It is because of that that God's chosen people came to be called Israelites. The Israelites were divided into twelve families or tribes, and each of these is descended from one of Jacob's twelve sons and is called by the name of that son. Jacob and his sons lived in Canaan until most of the family were grown up, and then they all went to Egypt. How that happened is a wonderful story; it is not in this book, because there are no angels in it.

The Israelites stayed in Egypt for nearly five hundred years. For a long time, they did very well there, but finally the king of Egypt, who was called Pharaoh, began to be frightened of them. They were hard-working people, very useful to him — but there were so many of them! God's promise to Abraham was coming true already; there were so many of them, they were very hard to count. Pharaoh wondered what would happen if all these people should revolt against him and try to take over his country. As often happens, being frightened made Pharaoh and the Egyptians cruel; they did everything they could to keep the Israelites busy earning just enough to eat, so that they would have no time left for anything else.

At last, God sent a man called Moses to bring them out of Egypt, and how he did it is another wonderful story that is not in this book. But he did bring them out at last into the desert beyond the Red Sea. They lived in this desert for forty years, and all that time, they had an angel to lead them where God wanted them to go. Then, at last, it was time for them to come home into the land God had given to Abraham and promised him his descendants should have for their own. That is why they called it the Promised Land. There were people living there already, people called Amorrhites and Moabites, and others, too. The Israelites had to fight for their country, but God was on their side.

The next story is about one of the things that happened when they were coming to take possession of their own Promised Land about twelve hundred years before our Lord was born.

Chapter Four

Balaam and Balac

When the Israelites came out of the desert at last, the power of God went with their armies, and no kingdom could withstand them. They conquered the Amorrhites and many of the Moabites, and when Og, king of Basan, marched out to meet them, they defeated him, too. And after that, they camped in the plains of Moab, across the river Jordan from Jericho.

Balac was a king in Moab who had had no dealings yet with the Israelites, but he could see their armies from the hills of his kingdom, and he did not like the look of them at all. He called some of the Madianite chiefs who were his neighbors to him and said, "These people are conquering all our neighbors as easily as an ox eats grass." And he sent the chiefs with a message to a soothsayer called Balaam.

Balaam lived some way away, on the borders of the country. This was the message from Balac: "There is a host of people on the march from Egypt. Their armies darken the earth, and they win all their battles. And now they are camped practically at my front door. Come and curse them for me, or they will conquer my kingdom. I know that you can curse people, and bless them, too." So the chiefs set out for Balaam's house with this message and all kinds of presents to pay him for his trouble.

When Balaam had read the message, he said to the chiefs, "Stay here tonight, and I will ask God what He wants me to do."

When the messengers slept, God came to Balaam, and Balaam said to Him, "Balac has sent me a message. He says a people has marched from Egypt whose armies darken the earth and who win all their battles. He wants me to go and curse them for him, so that he will be able to win a great victory over them. What shall I do?"

"Do not go with these messengers," said God, "and do not curse these people. My blessing goes with them."

Next morning, Balaam told the messengers he was sorry, but they must go home alone; God had told him not to go with them.

When Balac heard this news, he sent a fresh lot of messengers, greater chiefs than the first ones, and this was the message he sent with them: "Come to me as fast as you can, Balaam. I will give you high honors and anything else you want; only come and curse these people for me."

When Balaam had read this, he said, "Even if King Balac were to fill his house with gold and silver and give it to me, I could not disobey God. But stay here with me tonight, and I will see what the Lord says this time."

That night, God came to Balaam and said, "Go with them, but do not forget you are to say only what I tell you." Although God gave Balaam leave to go, He was not at all pleased with him, because He knew Balaam wanted to go for the sake of the fine presents Balac would give him.

Next morning, Balaam saddled his ass and set out with Balac's messengers. As he rode cheerfully along, thinking of all the lovely things Balac would give him, his ass suddenly slipped away, off the road into the open fields. Balaam was astonished; he had not seen what the ass had seen: an angel with a drawn sword standing in the middle of the road! He hit the ass and made her get back onto the road again.

All went well until they came to a place where the road ran between the walls of two vineyards. Here the ass saw the angel again and drew back against one of the walls, hurting Balaam's foot. Balaam hit her again.

The angel moved to a place where the road was very narrow, between rocky cliffs. There was no room at all to pass the angel, so the ass lay down. She couldn't think what else to do. Balaam was terribly angry; he hit her hard to make her get up again.

Then God gave the ass power to speak.

"This is the third time you have hit me," she said. "What have I done to deserve it?"

Balaam was in such a rage, he didn't notice for the moment how odd it was that his ass should be speaking to him. "You deserve it for the way you are behaving," he shouted. "If I had my sword here, I would kill you!"

"Why," said the ass, "you know me well enough; you have ridden me for years. Did I ever play you such a trick before?"

"Never —" said Balaam and then he looked up, and God let him see the angel standing in his path, still with the sword in his hand. Balaam was so frightened, he tumbled off the ass and lay face down on the road.

"What do you mean by beating your ass?" said the angel. "If she had tried to pass me, I would have killed you and spared her. I came to speak to you because you are going on this journey to please yourself, not to please God."

"I am sorry," said Balaam. "If you say so, I will go home again."

"No," said the angel. "Go on. But be careful to say no word when you reach Balac except what God tells you to say."

So Balaam got back on the ass, and away they went. What the chiefs thought of all this we don't know; probably they just thought Balaam was having trouble with his ass and had had a fall, and seemed to have been talking to himself.

When Balac heard that his messengers were coming back, and Balaam with them, he went out to meet them. "Why didn't you come the first time I sent for you?" he said when they met. "Did you think I wouldn't be able to reward you properly for your trouble?"

And Balaam answered, "I have come now, as you see. But I can say nothing except the words God puts in my mouth."

In the morning, Balac took Balaam up a hill from which he could see the nearest part of the army of the Israelites. First, Balaam said, seven altars must be built there and a ram and an ox offered in sacrifice on each. When that was done, he said, "Wait here by the altars, while I go apart and see if God will give me a message."

No sooner had Balaam walked away by himself than God met him. This is what He told Balaam to say when he went back: "I have come from my home, summoned by Balac, to curse the armies invading this country. How can I curse when God does not? Here is a people who dwell apart, sons of Israel, uncountable as the grains of sand on the seashore. May death find me as faithful as they are!"

Balac was not at all pleased. "What sort of trick is this?" he said. "I sent for you to curse my enemies, and it sounds as if you are blessing them instead."

"What else can I do?" said Balaam. "I can say only what God tells me to."

"Well, we'll try again, from another place," said Balac. "You can see too many of the Israelites from this hill." He took Balaam to another mountain, and there they built seven altars and offered seven rams and seven bullocks all over again.

And of course, it was no use.

43

"Stand there, Balac, and listen!" said Balaam. "God must fulfill His promises to this people of His. God is with them. He dwells in their camp. His trumpets sound for their victories. He has made them as strong as the wild ox."

"Oh, do be quiet!" said Balac.

"Didn't I warn you," said Balaam, "that I must say what God tells me to?"

"Well, all right," said Balac, a man who did not give up an idea easily. "We'll try one more place." He took Balaam to yet another mountain from which he could see the hosts of Israel. And they built seven altars and offered seven rams and seven bullocks on them all over again.

Then the spirit of God came down on Balaam, and he prophesied: "How lovely, Jacob, are your tents! How fair your dwellings! God has rescued you from Egypt, and you shall crush your enemies. A blessing on all who bless you; a curse on all who curse you!"

At that, Balac clapped his hands together in vexation. "That's the third time you have blessed my enemies," he said, "instead of cursing them. Go home, for goodness' sake. I meant to reward you and give you great honors. This God you serve has spoiled all your chances."

"I warned you," said Balaam, "that I could say only what God told me to. I said, 'Although Balac should fill his house with gold and silver and give it to me, I can give him only the message that God gives me for him.' "

And he got back on his patient ass and rode home.

Chapter Five

Tobias and the Angel

Canaan, the country God had given to Abraham to belong to his descendants forever, seemed a very large country to give to one man, but it wasn't really very big. In fact, as countries go, it was small. And although there seemed to be a terrific amount of people all descended from Abraham, Isaac, and Jacob, they were still not nearly so many as the people in some of the big countries around them. There was Egypt to the south of them, where they had lived for so long, under the Egyptians' power. And there was Babylonia on the east, and Assyria to the north. These were all great and powerful countries. Any of them could have swallowed up the little country they called the Promised Land overnight, if God had not been watching over His own people all the time.

But as long as His people obeyed Him and did not worship imitation gods, God kept them safe, and no armies could defeat them. The trouble was that they kept forgetting about their own God and worshiping the idols of the people among whom they lived. It is odd, but they would do it. When God thought they must really have a lesson, He would let them be attacked and defeated by one of these big countries. When that happened, many of them were carried off as prisoners by the people who had conquered them. They were put to work in the country they had been taken to, and sometimes they did quite well.

And if they did not understand why they had been defeated, God sent a man to tell them why it had happened, and to promise that if they would go back to worshiping their own God, He would bring them home again at last. These men with messages from God were called prophets. And the Chosen People who were taken away to strange countries were used by God to spread the knowledge of Him in places that would never have heard of Him otherwise.

The next three stories are about Jews taken away as captives, one to Assyria and the other two to Babylon.

About eight hundred years before our Lord grew up in Galilee, a Jew lived there whose name was Tobias. At that time, the king of the Jews was Jeroboam, and he was one of their worst kings. Instead of worshiping the true God, he worshiped idols and wanted everyone else to do so, too. His favorite kind of idol was a statue of a golden calf. There were golden calves all over the place, and many of Tobias's friends and acquaintances were quite ready to worship them and forget all about their own religion that had been given them by God. But Tobias would have nothing to do with golden calves; he stuck to worshiping God and went to the Temple in Jerusalem to do it, too. In everything, he kept the law of God as well as he could, even when he was a boy.

When he grew up, he married a girl called Anna. They had only one child, a son, whom they called Tobias after his father; they called him Toby, for short, because two people with the same name in one family is so confusing.

There they lived, very happily, in Galilee, until Shalmaneser the king of the Assyrians, made war on their country. He swept down on Galilee with his army and carried off many people as prisoners. Tobias and Anna and little Toby were all made prisoner by him and taken away to Niniveh in Assyria.

There, Tobias kept God's law and did his best to help other prisoners who were worse off than he was. God was very pleased with Tobias, and He made King Shalmaneser notice him and like him and even make a friend of him. The king let him travel around the country so that he could give to the other Jews who had been brought to Assyria help and good advice about how to get work and how to help themselves along. He gave food and clothes to those who needed them, and showed them how they could manage their affairs without offending God or the king. The king liked Tobias better and better and used to give him money to help him in all he was doing.

On one of his journeys, Tobias came to a city called Rages. (The odd name of this city has nothing to do with getting angry; it just happens to sound like our word *rage*.) Tobias had a large sum of money the king had given him. In Rages he found a man he knew, Gabelus, who wanted to start a business, but had no money. So Tobias lent him all the money the king had given him, and Gabelus was delighted. He gave Tobias a note, called a bond, that said he would repay the money one day, when Tobias asked for it. Gabelus knew he could do well once he got started.

Things were going quite nicely for Tobias and for the other Jews in Assyria at that time. But then King Shalmaneser died, and his son Sennacherib came to the throne.

Sennacherib hated all Jews. He made war against their country, as his father had done, and was defeated, which, of course, made him hate them all the more. When he got home again, furious because he had not won, he took his revenge on the Jews in Assyria.

Tobias suddenly found that things were worse than ever, just when he thought everything was settling down. Sennacherib and his soldiers killed Jews on any excuse at all and left their bodies where they had died, instead of burying them properly. Tobias went on with his work of helping Jews in need, but now there was something else he felt he must do, and that was to bury those poor men who were killed and left in the street or the fields. After people are dead, their bodies ought, of course, to be put tidily away in the earth. So whenever Tobias heard of a

Jew lying unburied, he went and got the body and took it home and, after dark, buried it.

Sennacherib, really a very unpleasant man, wanted the bodies left where they were as a warning to anyone who didn't dislike Jews as much as he did, so he was furious when he heard what Tobias was doing. He gave orders that Tobias and his family were to be put to death and their house and all that belonged to them seized. But Tobias heard what was going to happen, and he and Anna and Toby got away safely. Sennacherib took their property; the three of them had nothing but the clothes they wore.

Tobias had been kind to so many people that he found plenty of friends who would be kind to him and his family now. And only forty days later, Sennacherib was murdered by one of his own sons! After that, Tobias was able to come back to his own house, and his property was given back to him. It looked as if this new king would not be so bad, although it is hard really to like a king who comes to the throne by murdering his father. But things did not remain peaceful for long.

On the next Jewish feast day, Tobias planned to have a party, and he sent Toby to invite some of his relations. But Toby had hardly set out when he came running home to say that there was the body of a murdered Jew lying out in the street. Tobias jumped up at once, went and wrapped the body in a sheet and brought it home to his house, so that he could bury it after dark.

When his neighbors heard of this, they shook their heads and said, "You have only just escaped the death sentence for doing this very thing, and now are you going to start all over again?"

But Tobias feared God more than he feared the king. He not only buried that body, but whenever he heard of another, which was all too often, he did the same thing again.

One hot morning, he came home all worn out from grave digging, lay down on the shady side of his house, and fell asleep. While he was asleep, swallows who were building a nest under the eaves of his house dropped dung into his eyes, and when he woke up, he found he was blind.

"This is what comes of all your trying to please God," said his neighbors. "All your kindness and burying of the dead have brought you this reward: blindness!"

But Tobias thanked God every day that he was at least alive.

Meantime, Anna was worried about how they were to live, now that her husband could do nothing. Toby was just grown up, but he couldn't earn enough for the whole family, so Anna went to work. She wove cloth for neighbors who had looms and wanted cloth woven. For payment she accepted whatever they gave her. It might be loaves of bread, or eggs, or even money; whatever it was, it all helped. One day, she was given a young goat as payment, and when Tobias heard it bleating, he was suddenly frightened about what she might be doing. "You didn't steal that goat, did you?" he said to Anna.

"Indeed I didn't!" said Anna. "Steal indeed! When I work my hands to the bone every day for you! That is what all your giving away of our money has led to: hard work for me — and now you accuse me of stealing!"

Anna was as good as gold, really, and loved her husband and Toby, but she was tired and cross that evening, and to be accused of running off with someone's goat was the last straw!

That night, Tobias made a special prayer to God. "I know we are all sinners," he said, "and that I have deserved to be blind. But if you do not mean to forgive me and let me see again, please let me die."

⌒

Far away, in a city in Media, on that very same night, another special prayer was made to God. This one was made by a girl called Sara. She was a good and gentle Jewish girl, but the most extraordinary things kept happening to her. She had been married seven times, and each time, only a few hours after the wedding, her husband died. Each one was killed by a devil, but it was no fault of Sara's; she couldn't imagine what was happening. Her father, Raguel, was a cousin of Tobias and, like him, a very good man. He was just as puzzled as Sara.

On this particular night, when Sara made her special prayer, she was feeling very sad. In the morning of that day, she had told one of her mother's maidservants that something was not properly cleaned, and the maid had answered, "Well! So do you mean to murder me as you did all your husbands?" Sara was so horrified that she went straight to her room and stayed there, and that night she made this prayer to God: "Free me from this suspicion that I killed those poor men who married me, or let me die, too!"

Her prayer and the prayer of Tobias both reached the bright presence of God, and He sent Raphael, one of His holy angels, to help them both.

Meantime, old Tobias, thinking God was more likely to answer his prayer by letting him die than by giving back his sight, called Toby to him. He told Toby always to look after his mother, never to forget God, to give much to people in need when he had much to give, and if he had very little, to share that. Then he told Toby about the money he had lent to Gabelus and said that the time had come to collect the debt. The money would support Toby and his mother for a long time; Tobias wanted him to set out at once to find Gabelus in the city of Rages.

"Father, I will do my best," said Toby, "but how am I to find this city? Why, it must be two weeks' march away! Besides, it was so long ago that you lent Gabelus the money. What if he is dead, or has forgotten all about it, or does not believe I am your son?"

"I have Gabelus's bond here," said his father, "signed by him. Show him that, and he will give you the money at once. And as to how you are to find Rages, you must look for some responsible man who will show you the way for a reward. Start at once — do you want me to die before you have gone there and back?"

Poor Toby went out, wondering how in the world he was supposed to find someone who would go on such a journey with him. To his surprise, he saw a strange young man standing at the door. He was tall and handsome and all dressed for a journey. Toby greeted him politely and asked him where he came from.

"I have been among the men of Israel," the stranger said.

"Oh," said Toby. "Then perhaps you know the way to the city of Rages."

"I know it very well," said the stranger. "I have a friend there called Gabelus. I am on my way to visit him now."

"Please wait here just a moment," said Toby, all excited, "while I tell my father about this."

Old Tobias was very much astonished when he heard about this stranger who was on his way to visit the very man he wanted Toby to go and see.

"Bring him in at once!" he said. So Toby brought the stranger in, and he politely wished happiness to old Tobias.

"Happiness!" said Tobias. "How can I be happy, sitting here in the dark all day?"

"Cheer up," said the stranger. "God means to give your sight back to you soon."

Tobias thought he said this just to be kind, so he went on, "Will you take my son with you to see Gabelus? I will reward you well."

"I will take him," said the stranger, "and bring him home again, too."

This seemed to Tobias too good to be true; he wondered who in the world this young man could be, and if he was really to be trusted.

"What is your name?" Tobias said. "And who is your father?"

"I am called Azarias," said the stranger, "and my father is called Ananias." *Azarias* means "God has brought aid," and *Ananias* means "God has been merciful." Both were fairly ordinary names; Tobias knew a man called Ananias and supposed this must be his son. The answer set his mind at rest and, all arrangements having been made, he and Anna said goodbye to Toby.

"God be with you on your journey," said old Tobias, "and may His angel bear you company."

Toby and Azarias set off together down the road, and Anna cried to see them go. "I wish you had never owned that money," she said. "It was worth all the riches in the world to have my Toby here with us."

"Dry your eyes," said Tobias. "He will come home safely; I am sure some good angel is going with him and that all will be well."

Toby walked along happily, his dog at his heels and Azarias beside him. They took their first rest by the river Tigris, and Toby walked into the water to wash the dust off his feet. As he was paddling about, a very large fish came up as if it meant to bite him.

"Help!" shouted Toby. "There's a terrible fish here!"

"Catch it by the gill," said Azarias, "and pull it out of the water."

Toby plucked up his courage, seized the fish, and pulled it, flapping and struggling, up onto the bank.

"This is a very useful fish," said Azarias. "We will cook part of it now and salt the rest to carry on our journey. But save the liver and gall; both are wonderful remedies, and you will need them."

Toby cleaned the fish, carefully keeping the liver and gall. Afterward they made a fire and cooked their meal and rested a while before going on. Presently, as they were walking along the road again, Toby said, "Tell me, Azarias, what are the fish's gall and liver good for?"

"If you burn the liver," said Azarias, "the smoke will drive devils away. The gall is used for curing blindness."

"Ah!" thought Toby, "I must take that home for my father."

Each night on their long journey, they camped out in the open, or stayed with friends if there was anyone nearby whom Azarias knew. One day, as they set off in the morning, Toby said, "Where shall we stay tonight?"

"We shall visit a relation of yours whom you have never seen," said Azarias, "your cousin Raguel. He has a wife called Edna and one child, a girl called Sara. If you and Sara should marry, your father and hers would both be very pleased."

"Oh!" said Toby. "But I have heard of that girl! She has been married seven times, and each time the man who married her died a few hours after the wedding. If the story is true, it was a devil who killed them. My father and mother would certainly not like it if that happened to me!"

"The devil had power over those seven husbands," said Azarias, "because they had no love or fear of God. They married thinking only of getting a rich and beautiful wife for themselves. Over such men the devil has power. But if you marry Sara, you shall burn a piece of the fish's liver, and the smoke will drive the devil away. Besides that, you and she must spend the first three nights after the wedding in prayer. If you do this, all will be well."

That gave Toby plenty to think about for the rest of the day's march. When they arrived at Raguel's house, he and Edna came out to see who was there. "Why," said Raguel, looking at Toby, "did you ever see anyone so like my cousin Tobias? Look, Edna, isn't it astonishing how like my cousin he is? Where are you from, young man?"

"From Niniveh," said Toby rather absentmindedly, because he had just caught sight of Sara.

"From Niniveh!" said Raguel. "Why then, you must know my cousin! He is such a good man, such a wonderful man —"

"This is his son," said Azarias.

Raguel was simply delighted. He hugged Toby and kept telling him how happy he was to see him and how like his father he was, and what a great man his father was, and asking Edna if it wasn't the most wonderful surprise to see him, and so on. Toby answered politely, but he couldn't take his eyes off Sara. He thought she was the loveliest girl he had ever seen.

After they had all sat talking for a while, Raguel jumped up and said he must see about getting a sheep killed; they must have a great feast to honor his favorite cousin's son!

"Grant me a favor first," said Toby. "I will not feast with you unless you grant it. Please, may I marry Sara?"

Raguel was very much taken aback, as well he might be. Not only was it very sudden, but he remembered the seven bridegrooms who had all died a few hours after their wedding with Sara. While he was trying to think what to say, and, of course, not liking to mention the other bridegrooms, Azarias said, "Do not be afraid to grant his wish. He is the husband God intends for Sara; both of them will be safe and happy in His care."

"Why, then," said Raguel, "God has heard my prayers. He must have sent you here so that Sara would be the wife of my dear cousin's son." Everyone who heard Azarias speak was quite sure he knew what he was talking about and that he was telling the truth.

Then Raguel said to Toby, "She is yours," and he took Sara's hand and Toby's hand and joined them together. Sara does not seem to have had much to say about whether she wanted to marry Toby; but she made no difficulty about joining hands with him, so very likely she had been admiring him almost as much as he had her, although not so openly.

"May God be with you both," said Raguel. "And now we really will have a feast, and a wedding, too!"

After the wedding and while the feast was being cooked, Edna got the best spare room ready for Toby and Sara. She told Sara not to be afraid; she was sure this husband would not suddenly die, as the others had. "You have had enough sadness," she said. "Now I am sure God means you to be happy instead." But just the same, she cried all the time, as mothers often do at weddings.

When Toby and Sara went up to their room, Toby took a piece of the fish's liver and threw it on the fire, as Azarias had told him to do.

Meantime, Toby said to Sara, "Tonight and tomorrow night and the night after we must spend in prayer. Then God will bless our marriage, give us lovely children, and keep us safe in His care all our lives." So they knelt down together and kept a vigil all night long.

Toby prayed, "Lord God of our fathers, praise be to You from all the heavens and the earth and the seas and rivers and all the creatures that make their homes in them. May Your name be blessed forever."

Sara prayed, "Have mercy on us, Lord, have mercy on us. Keep us safe from harm, and let us grow old together, Toby and I."

They said many more prayers as the night went on and did not stop until they heard the first cock crow and knew the night was over. Then they both went to sleep.

Meantime, Raguel woke up and began thinking, "What if, after all, Toby is dead?" He, too, heard the first cock crow, and when he heard it, he got up and dressed. He crept out of the house, woke some of his farm men and told them to dig a grave — just in case! Then he went back and woke Edna, and told her to send one of the maids to Toby and Sara's room to see if all was well. Edna was afraid to go herself, in case Toby was dead. The maid opened the door softly and looked in, and there were Toby and Sara, both sound asleep. When she brought the news to Edna and Raguel, they thanked God with all their hearts. Then Raguel ran out and told his farm men to fill the grave up again quickly, before Toby or Sara came down and saw it!

Later that day, Raguel told Toby that he was giving Sara half of all his possessions for her dowry, and that he wanted Toby and Sara to stay with him at least two weeks longer. It would take some time to sort out half of everything, cattle and sheep and furniture, gold and silver and linen, not to mention Sara's own clothes and special belongings. Raguel wanted Toby there to help with all this, and also he didn't want to see his daughter go off so soon, and with a man he had met only the day before!

When Toby understood this, he took Azarias aside and said to him, "I can never possibly repay you for all you have done for me, and now instead of even trying to, I am going to ask you to do something more! Raguel wants me to stay here for two weeks longer, and I can see that I shall have to. But you know how worried my mother and father will be, for we shall be much longer getting home than we expected. So I wondered if you would go on to Gabelus for me, taking his bond, and collect the money he owes my father? Perhaps you could persuade him to return with you to share the last feast before we go."

Azarias was perfectly willing to do this, so away he went. Gabelus, who had grown rich since Tobias knew him, was delighted both to pay his debt and to come to Raguel's house to meet Toby and hear news of his father.

At the end of two weeks, when everything was ready, Raguel and Edna still did not want Toby to go. Toby said he really must, for he was expected already, and it would be nearly two weeks before he reached home. He knew Anna would think he had been robbed or murdered on the journey or had fallen ill, or that Gabelus had gone to another town and couldn't be found, or was dead. . . . And he was quite right: his mother was worried to death. She kept going up the hill behind the house and sitting on top of it, looking down the road to see if she could catch sight of Toby coming home. Poor Tobias couldn't even do that; he just sat at home and worried and told Anna not to worry.

It was indeed high time Toby went back, and at last he persuaded Raguel of it, and the whole party set out for Tobias's house. What with camels whose loads came off, and sheep not liking to be hurried, and cows wanting to eat grass by the road all the way, and bundles getting left behind where they had camped for the night, and the farm men stopping to argue about everything, and Sara's maidservant bursting into tears when she saw a little snake, Toby began to think they might as well have stayed with Raguel for all the progress they were making!

After some days of this, Azarias said to Toby, "I know how anxious your father must be. Wouldn't it be a good idea if you and I went on ahead as fast as we can, and left the rest to follow at their own pace?"

Toby thought that was a wonderful idea, so he said goodbye to Sara and, taking only a little food and the fish's gall, they set off as fast as they could walk, stopping only when they were too tired to go any further.

When they came in sight of Niniveh, Anna was sitting on the hilltop as usual; she saw them while they were still a long way off, and she knew at once who they were. How fast she ran down the hill and home! "Toby is coming!" she called to Tobias and at once began to bustle about, getting everything ready.

"When you get home," said Azarias to Toby, "thank God first for your safe return. Then, as soon as you have greeted your father, put the fish's gall on his eyes. In a little while, he will be able to see again."

Toby took the gall and ran on ahead, but even so, he was not the first to reach home! His dog ran faster and raced into the house, his tail going a mile a minute, and making those delighted noises dogs make when they see people they are fond of after a long time. When Tobias heard him and felt his tail wagging against his legs, he jumped up and ran for the door of the house, stumbling over the dog and everything else in his way. A servant ran to help him, caught him by the hand, and led him out of the house. By this time, Anna came running, too, and so Toby and his parents met on the path to the house, with the dog jumping around them, and a tremendous amount of hugging and crying going on.

At last, they all stood still for a minute and thanked God out loud that Toby had come safely home.

Then Toby, as he had been told, put the fish's gall on his father's eyes. "In a little while," he said, "you will be able to see." And after they had sat and talked for a while, before Toby had had time to tell them a quarter of his adventures, all of a sudden Tobias could see. They all thanked God again, as well they might, for His kindness to them.

"I thank You, Lord God," said Tobias, "because You punished me and now You have taken away the punishment! Oh, thank You, because I can see, and because one of the things I can see is my son, Toby, safe home again!" And they thanked Azarias, too, of course.

All the neighbors had heard the excitement by this time, and came to see what was going on. When they heard the news, they all joined in, in thanking God and congratulating Tobias. Sara, with all the farm stock and the carts and her father's servants, did not arrive until a week later. In the meantime, of course, Toby had told his mother and father all about her, and so she arrived to find still another wedding feast waiting for her.

But before she came, Tobias took his son aside and said, "How shall we pay Azarias for all he has done for us?"

"We can never possibly pay him enough," said Toby. "Why, he not only took me safely to Raguel's house, found me my darling wife, drove the devil away, collected your money from Gabelus, and saw me safely home; we owe the cure for your blindness to him, too! The very least we can do is to offer him half the wealth that has come to us through his means."

So they called Azarias to them and asked him to accept half of their new wealth for his reward. But he said, "Give all the thanks to God; it was not my idea that I should come and help you. It is God who has brought aid to you, God who has been merciful to you. I told you so, but you thought I was only telling you my name and my

65

father's name. What you must do in return is to praise God aloud so that everyone can hear you, and tell all that He has done for you. Kings have secrets that must not be told, but God's ways are open, and he honors God best who speaks openly of all God has done for him.

"You pleased God all your life, Tobias, by prayer and fasting and kindness; see what treasure you were laying up for yourself. Your kindness to people in want has kept death away from you, won you mercy, and will win you eternal life. Sinners win nothing; they are their own souls' enemies.

"And now it is time for you to be told the whole truth and to understand God's hidden purposes.

"When you, Tobias, prayed so hard to God, when you risked your life to give burial to the dead, I stood all the while in the presence of God, offering Him your prayers and good deeds. Although you had won His favor, He still allowed trials and sorrows to come to you, to test your worth. Then, for your healing, and for the deliverance of Sara, your son's wife, he chose to send me as His messenger.

"Who am I? I am Raphael; one of the seven angels who always stand in the presence of God."

When they heard this, Tobias and Toby were terrified and fell down with their faces to the ground. But Raphael said, "Peace be with you. Do not be afraid. Only remember, it was God's will that brought me to your help; pay Him the thanks and praise you owe Him. When you,

Toby, obeyed me and burned the fish's liver on your wedding night, it was I who pursued the devil who had been lying in wait for you. I caught him and made him my prisoner in the deserts of Upper Egypt, while you and Sara prayed. I have lived among you as if I were a man, but it was only outward show; the food I live by no eyes can see. And now the time has come when I must go back to Him who sent me. Give thanks to God, and tell the story of His great deeds."

No sooner had Raphael said this than he vanished from their sight. Tobias and Toby stayed where they were and thanked God for three hours together. Then they got up, and, as Raphael had told them to, they began to tell everyone what God had done for them; Tobias even made up a song about it.

Tobias lived a long time after this, long enough to see Toby's seven sons grow up and have children of their own. But that was nothing like so long as the time he has been in Heaven since he died.

Chapter Six

Daniel in Babylon

The furnace in this story was either a limekiln or an oven for baking bricks. It looked like a little square house with a door through which the bricks or the lime could be taken out when they were ready, and a large hole at the top into which the fuel was put. There were little square windows, too, through which air could go in to make the fire burn better. When the furnace was going really well, flames came out of these windows as well as out of the top.

The angels in this story are rather scattered, but you will see that one always turns up, just when he is most needed.

Six hundred years before our Lord was born, Nebuchadnezzar, the king of Babylon, laid siege to Jerusalem and took it. He carried off a great many captives. When he got back to Babylon, he told the man who looked after his household affairs to choose the best-looking and most intelligent of the Jewish boys among his prisoners, and have them educated. They were to spend three years learning the language and everything else that could be taught them. Then they were to be brought to the king, and he would ask them questions to see if he thought them worth having with him at court.

Four of the boys chosen were called Daniel, Hananiah, Mishael, and Azariah. But they were given new names in Babylon. Daniel's didn't stick very well; his new name was Belteshazzar, but people mostly went on calling him Daniel. The other three were called by their new names, which were Shadrach, Meshach, and Abednego.

These four settled down to school and learned all they could. They did not forget that they were Jews; they worshiped no God except their own, true God. They would have nothing to do with the idols that were worshiped in Babylon and always remembered their own prayers.

God was pleased about this and helped them to learn, so that at the end of three years, they knew more than the masters who had taught them.

When they were brought to the king, they answered his questions so well that he was delighted. He said they must all have places at court. God had made Daniel especially good at knowing what dreams meant, because He knew this would be a great help to him. The people in Babylon thought dreams were very important; they had special people whose business was to explain the meaning of people's dreams. The king was very pleased when he found out that Daniel understood dreams so well. He wanted to make him ruler of all the three parts of his kingdom. But Daniel persuaded him to give one part each to Shadrach, Meshach, and Abednego to rule, and to let him stay at court as the king's counselor.

Although the king liked Daniel so much, he had no idea what Daniel's God was like. He went on worshiping idols, as everyone else in his kingdom did. And, not content with the idols that were there already, he had a new one made. This was an enormous golden statue, ninety feet high and nine feet wide. When it was finished, it was set up in the plain outside the city, where everyone could see it. The king sent word to all the governors and magistrates and judges and everyone of any importance in his country, that they were all to come to the dedication of this idol. When they had all arrived, he sent a herald around, crying out, "As soon as the band begins to play, everyone is to fall down on his face and worship this golden statue. Whoever does not worship it will be thrown into a raging furnace."

As soon as the band began to play, down they all fell. All except the Jews, who had taken care to be somewhere else! But some of the people who were jealous of them came and said to the king, "O King, live forever! Do you know that those Jews you have made rulers of your provinces won't worship your beautiful idol?"

The king was furious when he heard this. He sent for Shadrach, Meshach, and Abednego and said, "So, you won't worship my statue? Either you do, or I will throw you into the furnace. You are in my power; what god can save you from me?"

The three answered, "You will see for yourself. But whether our God rescues us or not, we will never worship any other god but Him."

Nebuchadnezzar was not at all used to being talked to like that. He flew into a terrible rage and gave orders that the furnace was to be heated seven times more than usual. As soon as the fire was burning fiercely, the king's guards tied up the three Jews and threw them into it. The fire was so hot that the men who threw them in were burned to death.

But Shadrach, Meshach, and Abednego found that the fire did not burn them, or their clothes; it only burned off their bonds. They walked about, quite cool and happy, in the middle of the flames. Meantime, the king sat and watched the furnace and made his guards throw more and more fuel into the fire, so that immense flames came shooting up through the hole in the top of the furnace and through the windows.

Meanwhile, the three in the furnace found that there was a fourth person there. He was an angel, and it was he who drove the heat away and made a cool wind blow in the middle of the fire. It was then that the three sang a song which we still sing: "Bless the Lord, angels of the Lord! Bless the Lord, heavens and waters above the heavens! Bless the Lord, sun, moon, and stars! Bless the Lord, ice and snow, daytime and nighttime, bless the Lord! Bless the Lord, mountains and hills and everything that lives in the waters! Bless the Lord, flying birds and wild beasts and tame beasts, and all the men on the earth! Souls of all good men, bless the Lord!"

Meantime, King Nebuchadnezzar was sitting opposite the door to the furnace. He could see through it into the heart of the fire. And suddenly he jumped up. "Didn't we throw them in all tied up?" he said. "Three of them?"

"Of course we did," said his courtiers.

"But I can see four men in the fire," said the king, "and they are not tied up. They are walking about. And the fourth looks like a god."

With that, the king went near the door of the furnace and called, "Come out, Shadrach, Meshach, and Abednego, servants of the most high God!"

The three came out, and everyone crowded around to look. They were just as they had been before they went into the furnace, except there was no sign of the ropes they had been bound with. Their hair wasn't singed; their clothes didn't smell of fire; they weren't even too hot!

"Henceforward," said the king, "no one is to say a word against the God of these people."

We don't know where Daniel was when all this was going on, but we do know that he went on serving the king, and that the king went on being pleased with him. He told the king what his dreams meant, even when they meant something very unpleasant. One dream said that the king was going to go mad and live in the fields for seven years, eating grass, like a cow. And it happened, too! But the king still loved Daniel.

After he died, King Belshazzar reigned, and for him, too, Daniel interpreted dreams.

~

But there came a day when King Belshazzar made a great feast for a thousand of the greatest men in his kingdom. In the middle of it, when everyone had had rather too much wine to drink, he had an idea. "Fetch me the gold and silver cups that Nebuchadnezzar brought back from the Temple in Jerusalem!" he said. "We will all drink our wine from those." This was like taking the chalice used at Mass to serve drinks at a party — a dreadful thing to do. But Belshazzar and his guests thought it a great joke. They drank from the cups and got more drunk and noisy than ever.

And it was then that the king looked up at the wall of the banqueting hail and saw a terrible thing. The fingers of a hand were writing on the wall. There was nothing else to be seen: no hand and arm, no one there, just fingers writing words on the wall.

The king lost his gaiety all of a sudden and cried out and pointed. Everyone saw the fingers then and watched in terror as they moved across the wall.

Then the king called for all the wise men in the kingdom to come and read what the fingers had written, for no one there could read it. But when the wise men came, they couldn't read the words either. "The man who reads me what is written there," said the king, "shall be dressed in a robe of royal purple with a gold chain around his neck, and shall hold the third place in my kingdom."

But still they couldn't read it. All this excitement brought the king's mother down to the banqueting hall to find out what was going on. When she was shown the writing and told no one could read it, she said, "Why, Daniel is the man you want. He is a man inspired by the gods; King Nebuchadnezzar would have sent for him before this."

So Daniel was brought to the hall and asked to read what was written. The king promised again that, if he could read the writing, he should have a royal robe and a gold chain and be the third man in the kingdom.

"Keep your robe and chain," said Daniel, "and give honors to anyone else you please. I will read what is written, but you will not like it. All your life you have worshiped idols and paid no heed to the true God, and now you have taken the cups from His Temple to use at your feast. That is why this message has come to you. This is what is written: MANE, THECEL, PHARES. *Mane* means numbering: so many years God has allowed you to rule, and now they have ended. *Thecel* means weighing: your good deeds weigh too light, your evil deeds too heavy. *Phares* means tearing: your kingdom is going to be torn out of your grasp."

When the king had heard this, he ordered a royal robe to be put on Daniel and a gold chain around his neck and had it proclaimed that he was now the third greatest man in his kingdom, just as he had sworn to do. But that night Belshazzar was killed and his kingdom brought to an end.

As *angel* means messenger, and the words written on the wall were a message from God, we can only suppose it was an angel who wrote them, although the fingers of the hand were all that could be seen.

⌒

It was the Persians who conquered Belshazzar's kingdom, and the new king they set to rule over it was called Darius. He honored Daniel, too, and put him in charge of one-third of his kingdom. The two men who ruled the other two-thirds were not nearly as good at it as Daniel, and the king thought of putting him to rule all three.

But the friends of the other two rulers were jealous and plotted to get rid of Daniel altogether. They came to the king and said, "Will you do us a favor? It is not one that will be any trouble to you! Make a law that, for the next month, no one is to pray to any god or man for anything at all, but for all they need, they are to ask you. And make it the law that if anyone disobeys this rule, he is to be thrown into the lions' pit."

Darius thought it an odd request, but he saw no harm in it, and he made the law as they asked. But when Daniel heard of it, he understood at once that his enemies meant to report to the king that he was saying prayers to his God every day. But he didn't stop praying because of that. He used to open the window of his room that faced toward the east, where Jerusalem was, and there, at morning and midday and night, he said his prayers.

As soon as the plotters were sure he was still doing this, they went running to the king. "Daniel is praying to his God!" they said. "He has disobeyed your law. You must give him to the lions, as you promised."

King Darius didn't want to do this at all. He thought all day how he could get around the law he had made, but it was no use. The Medes and Persians were very proud of never, never altering a law once the king had signed it.

At last, the king, seeing there was no help for it, ordered Daniel to be thrown into the lions' den. "You are so faithful to your God," he said to Daniel. "Surely He will help you now." Then he set his seal across the edge of the stone that shut the door of the den, and the men who had plotted against Daniel did the same, feeling very pleased with themselves!

But the king could eat no supper that night, and he couldn't sleep. Very early in the morning, he went out to the lion pit and called out, "Daniel, worshiper of the living God, and His true servant, are you safe?"

"Long live the king!" Daniel called out cheerfully from among the lions. "An angel came to look after me. How could any harm come to me, when God knows I am innocent?"

The king was delighted. He had Daniel taken out of the pit at once, and those who had plotted against him were thrown in instead. The lions ate them up in a moment.

Then Darius made another law, that no one was ever again to say a word against Daniel's God. And that law, like the first one, could not be changed!

Daniel was given wonderful visions of the times to come, but they are very hard to understand. The archangel Gabriel, looking like a man, came and spoke to him, too. So did another angel who, he said, was "dressed in white linen, with a golden belt. And his eyes shone like candles and lightning seemed to play about his head, and his skin had the gleam of bronze."

This angel spoke to him about the archangel Michael and told him that Michael was the guardian of the Jewish race. So if you have any Jewish friends, it is a good idea to pray to Michael for them. It's nice to know that peoples and countries have guardian angels as well as each of us.

In between his visions, Daniel was still the king's counselor. The last king he served was called Cyrus. This king loved him just as the others had done, but he was not a very bright king, as you will see.

Cyrus, like everyone else in Babylon, except the Jews, still worshiped idols. One of his favorite idols was called Bel. Bel was an enormous statue with a temple all to himself and seventy priests to serve him.

Every day great sacks of flour, forty sheep, and thirty-six extra-large bottles of wine were brought to the temple for Bel's dinner. The seventy priests made loaves of bread with the flour, roasted the sheep, and set out the food and wine on a great table in front of the statue of Bel.

The king asked Daniel one day why he wouldn't worship Bel like everyone else.

"I worship only the living God who made the whole world," said Daniel.

"What!" said Cyrus. "Can't you see that Bel is a living god? Why, look what an appetite he has; see how much food he eats every day!"

"Oh, my lord king!" said Daniel. "Do not believe such stories! Bel is made of metal on the outside and clay on the inside; he cannot possibly eat."

That made the king think. He called Bel's priests to him and said, "Prove to me that Bel eats the food provided for him every day. If you cannot prove it, you shall all be killed. If you can prove it, Daniel shall die instead."

"Just as you please," said Daniel.

Next day, Daniel and the king went to Bel's temple, and the high priest said, "Now, King Cyrus, we are all going to leave the temple. It will be for you to set the table for Bel today and pour his wine. When everything is in readiness, go out and shut the doors and put your seal across the crack. Tomorrow morning, come back and see if Bel has not eaten everything."

They went away, and the king and his servants set Bel's dinner out for him. When all was ready, but before the door was sealed, Daniel sent his servants to sprinkle fine white ashes all over the floor. If the king wondered what was going on, he said nothing.

Next morning, they came back to the temple again, and the king said, "Well, Daniel, is my seal broken?"

"No," said Daniel, "it is just as we left it."

They opened the door, and the king gave a shout. "You are a real god with a real appetite, Bel!" he cried, for he could see that there was not a scrap of food or a drop of wine left!

But Daniel was smiling. "Do not go in yet," he said to the king, "but look at the floor."

"Why," said the king, staring in astonishment, "I can see footprints all over the place. Men and women and little children have been here since we left!" The ashes Daniel had had spread over the floor showed up the footprints beautifully; he could hardly keep from laughing.

The king flew into a terrible rage and had all the seventy priests of Bel put into prison. Soon enough, one of them confessed that they had a secret entrance to the temple, close under Bel's dining table. All seventy of them, and their wives and children, too, used to come through it every night and eat up Bel's dinner. The king was so angry at the trick they had played on him that he ordered all of them to be put to death immediately. And he told Daniel he could do as he pleased with Bel and his temple, too. So Daniel destroyed them both.

But if the king was not going to worship Bel anymore, he was not going to worship the true God, either. He said to Daniel, "You were right about Bel being made of nothing but metal and clay, but we have a living god, too. He is a great snake. You must worship him with us, for you cannot say that he is not alive."

"He is alive all right," said Daniel, "but he isn't a god. If you will give me leave, I will kill him without using a sword or a club or any weapon."

"Try then," said the king.

Daniel boiled an awful pudding of pitch and fat and hair and fed it to the snake. And the snake happily swallowed it, and burst in the middle, and died.

"Look at your god now," said Daniel.

This was all very well, but the people of Babylon were furious. A great crowd of them stormed the palace and demanded to see the king. When they saw him, they said, "Are you a Jew, like Daniel? You have overthrown Bel and killed his priests and destroyed his temple, and now our snake-god is killed, too! It is all Daniel's fault. Give him up to us, or we will kill you and all your servants!"

The king was scared out of his wits, and although he hated to do it, he gave Daniel up to them. And what did they do to Daniel? Threw him into the lions' pit, of course! Daniel must have thought, "Here we go again!" as he went in. They planned to leave him there for a week and to give the lions nothing to eat all that time, so that they would be quite certain to eat Daniel.

In the meantime, far away in Judea, an old prophet called Habacuc had been cooking. He was a farmer as well as a prophet, and at this time, he had men reaping in his fields. So he had cooked a meal for them. It was a great bowl of broth with plenty of bread crumbled into it. Just as he was carrying it out to them, an angel spoke to him. "Take this dinner to Daniel," said the angel. "He is in the lions' den in Babylon."

"Lord," said Habacuc, "I have never been in Babylon in my life, and I don't know anything about a lions' den there." Before he could say another word, the angel caught him by the hair and carried him through the air to Babylon. All in a moment, he found himself standing by the entrance to the lions' den. So, very surprised, but with his wits about him, he called out, "Daniel! The Lord has sent you your dinner; come and take it."

So Daniel, very grateful to God for remembering him, and very hungry, too, reached up through the barred entrance to the pit and took the bowl from Habacuc.

As for Habacuc, the angel took him by the hair again, and all at once he was set down beside his own door. Let us hope he had some more broth and bread for the reapers!

When Daniel had been in the lions' den for a week, the king went to look in at the lions. He was very sorry Daniel should have been killed, but did not see how he could have prevented it. He was really a very silly king. But when he looked into the pit, there was Daniel sitting among the lions, not hurt at all.

"How great Daniel's God is!" said the king. And then, plucking up his courage, he had Daniel taken out of the pit and the leaders of the people who had put him there were given to the lions instead. They were eaten up in a moment; the poor lions were so hungry.

"The whole world ought to worship Daniel's God," said the king, who seems to have really gotten the idea at last. "He is a God who can keep a man safe even in a den of lions!"

Chapter Seven

Cherubim and Seraphim

E zekiel was carried off to Babylon a few years later than
Daniel. He was not sent to school like Daniel because he was quite grown up and was a priest of the true
God besides. He was sent instead to live in the country
on the banks of the Grand Canal. A lot of Israelites were
settled there. While he was there, God showed him why
he had been carried off. God wanted the Jews in exile to
have a prophet among them, and Ezekiel was to be the
prophet. A prophet, of course, is a man whom God uses
to give people messages from Him.

Ezekiel wrote down the story of what happened to
him, just as it is here, except that in the Bible there is a
lot more of it.

He saw the most extraordinary vision of angels of the
kind called cherubim. They were making a sort of chariot
for the throne of God. It was rather like seeing a picture
on the sky. This is quite different from seeing an angel
walking about on the earth looking like a man.

The mountain east of the Temple in the story is Mount
Olivet, from which our Lord went back to Heaven.

Adonis is a made-up god who was supposed to be born every spring and die in the heat of summer. So people worshiping him sat and wept when the weather got hot, because poor Adonis was dying. It seems terribly silly, but they really did.

An inkhorn was a real animal's horn, with a top fitted onto it. People who did a lot of writing used to carry ink like that, just as, long afterward, hunters and soldiers used powder horns to carry gunpowder for their guns.

⌒

Ezekiel's Story

I was living with the exiles by the Grand Canal when Heaven opened, and I saw a vision of God. A stormy wind had sprung up and was blowing from the north. A great dark cloud was driven before the wind, and in the midst of the cloud, there seemed to be fire, and it was edged with brightness. And I saw, there in the heart of the cloud, in the fiery part, an amber-colored glow. And there were living people there.

They seemed to be men, but each had four faces and two pairs of wings. Their legs were straight and ended in hoofs like the hoofs of calves, and these sparkled like red-hot bronze. Their arms, showing under their wings, were like men's arms. Each held two wings across his body and flew with the other two. When they moved, they went all together and straight ahead, never turning. Each had the face of a man in front, but seen from the right, each looked like a lion, from the left like an ox, and from above like an eagle.

Going to and fro in the midst of them was a glow like fire, and from this lightning came out.

I stood watching these living people come and go, bright as lightning flashes. And as I watched, all at once I saw great wheels beside them, one at each of the four sides. All the wheels were of the color of sea water, and each had another wheel inside it, a wheel within a wheel. These moved as the living people did, always straight forward. Their height was terrible to see, and the rims of them were all full of eyes.

When the living people moved, the sound of their wings was like the sound of a river in flood, or thunder, or the murmur of voices from a great crowd. The sound stopped only when they were still. Over the living people a high arch seemed to rise like a sheet of dazzling crystal resting on their heads. Above this arch of crystal, sapphire blue towered up in the shape of what seemed to be a throne, and there was someone there, above the throne. All about Him was amber-colored flame. Upward and downward from His waist, light like a rainbow shone; there was brightness all about Him.

So much I saw of what the glory of the Lord is like, and seeing it, I fell face down on the ground.

Then I heard a Voice that said to me, "Rise up, son of man. I have something to say to you." At these words, I was strengthened so that I could stand up and listen.

"Son of man," the Voice said, "I am sending you to the men of Israel. They have forsaken me and rebelled against me. You are to give them this message, whether they will listen to you or not. At least they are to know that they have a prophet among them. Do my bidding, son of man. Open your mouth, and eat what I give you."

With that, I saw a hand stretched out, with a book in it. When the book was opened, I saw that everything written in it was about sorrow and misery.

"Eat this book," said the Voice of God, and I opened my mouth and ate the book. It tasted sweet as honey.

"Now," said the Voice, "go to your fellow exiles and give them my message."

Then there was a great stir of the living figures and a whirring of wings and wheels as the vision moved onward. I set out to return to the exiles among whom I lived.

For seven days I could not speak to them; I was worn out and full of sorrow.

Then the word of the Lord came to me again, and He told me to get a tile and draw a picture on it. The picture was to be of Jerusalem. He told me also to get an iron cooking pot and bury it so that only the rim showed above the earth. And I was to set the tile in this, so that the rim surrounded it like an iron wall.

"Here, you are to tell them," said the Voice of God, "is the siege of Jerusalem. It will be as impossible to break through as this iron rim. It is Nebuchadnezzar who will besiege the city, and it will fall. It will fall because my people who live there have forsaken me."

All this I did, and many more signs that the Lord told me to do, but few listened to me or attended. They said I spoke only in parables, but all they meant was that they did not want to understand. But God told me still to prophesy doom to them, whether they would listen to me or not.

Then one day, when I sat in my house among my friends, the power of God came over me again. A man appeared who seemed made of fire and amber light. A hand caught me by a lock of my hair and lifted me between Heaven and earth, and I was carried away to Jerusalem.

I stood by the gateway leading to the main court of the Temple. The bright presence of God was there, too, as I had seen it by the Grand Canal. "Son of man," I heard His Voice say, "look."

And I looked and saw an idol standing in the very doorway of the Temple of God. "Wicked deeds are done here," said the Voice of God. "Little wonder if I go away from my holy place when my own people do me such wrong. But you have worse to see."

With that, He brought me close to the door of the court where there was a hole in the wall. It seemed in my vision that I was to dig the hole larger and go through it. I did that and found myself opposite a door. "Go in," said the Voice of God, "and see what is being done here in my Temple."

I opened the door and went through, and what did I see but paintings of snakes and animals: pictures of all the gods that wicked Jews worship. And in front of them stood seventy of the chief men of Israel, each with a censer offering incense to them, so that the place was full of smoke.

"Now," said the Voice of God, "you have seen what the chief men in Israel are doing, here in the darkness. 'We need not fear the Lord,' they say. 'He will not see us; He has forsaken us for good and all.' And there is more yet for you to see." He took me through another gate of the Temple, and there I saw women sitting, weeping for Adonis!

"There is worse yet," said the Voice of God, and He took me into the inner part of the Temple, the holy place of God, and there between the porch and the altar stood five and twenty men. They were facing outward, looking at the sky, not the altar. They were worshiping the sun!

"Have you seen enough of what is being done in my house?" said the Voice of God. "They are busy with their wickedness, and I will be busy with my vengeance at last."

Then I heard His Voice cry aloud, "Make way for the plagues that must fall on the city!"

And I saw six men coming, all armed, and in the midst of them a man dressed in linen. This man carried an inkhorn at his belt, as writers do. These seven stood ready by the altar, and the glory of God towered high up above the threshold. He summoned the man in linen and told him to walk all through Jerusalem. Wherever he found good men who were truly sorry about the idols in the Temple and who feared God and wished to please Him, he was to mark their foreheads with a cross. And the six armed men He told to follow behind him, killing all those who were not marked with a cross. And in my vision I saw that all this was done; the wicked were killed, beginning with the idolaters in the Temple.

And I, standing among all that death and ruin, cried out, "Alas, alas, Lord God! Will You destroy even the few who are left of Israel, pour Your destruction over the whole land?"

"Shall I be sorry for them?" said the Voice of God. "When they have filled the city and the country with murder and all kinds of wickedness?"

And I saw the man in linen come back. He stood before the throne of God and said, "I have done what You sent me to do." Then I looked up and up, above the arch of crystal to the sapphire blue that towered up like a throne, and I heard the Voice of God say to the man in linen, "Make your way in among the cherubim. Take a handful of hot coals from among them, and pour these over the city."

I watched him make his way among the cherubim, the living beings; they were close to the right side of the Temple. He stood by the whirring wheels, and one of the cherubim left the others and reached into the flames. He brought out a handful of hot coals and gave them to the man in linen, who went on his way.

Then I saw the cherubim and the bright presence of God rise up and leave the Temple and come to rest at the eastern gate, and I, too, was taken there.

Here I saw twenty-five men talking together. "Son of man," said the Voice of God, "these men are plotting mischief; they mean to give the city bad advice. Tell them of their doom, son of man."

Then I spoke aloud in my vision, warning the men who were plotting of the destruction I had seen, the destruction that was to come upon the city. And I told them it was to happen because they had forsaken God and turned to idols instead.

So I prophesied, and while I spoke, one of the men dropped down dead. Then I fell on my face on the ground and cried out to God, "Alas, alas, Lord God! Will you destroy us all?"

But His Voice answered, "You have brothers still, son of man; you have brothers still. Your nearest kin are those far away, the exiled sons of Israel, those who are scattered far from my holy Temple. They shall find a little holy place in my friendship. Tell them this, from me, the Lord God: 'You are lost among the peoples of the world, but I will find you. I will give you this land again for your home, and you shall have new hearts that will turn to me.' In those days, they shall do as I tell them, and they shall be my people, and I will be their God. It is only the men whose hearts are set in wickedness who will be punished."

And now the cherubim spread their wings for flight, the wheels beside them and the bright presence of God above them, and that presence, going away from the Temple and the city, rested for a moment on the mountain to the east of Jerusalem. With that, the vision faded from my eyes, and I found myself back among the exiles on the banks of the Grand Canal.

I told them all the Lord had shown me.

Sure enough, Jerusalem fell to the king of Babylon, and he destroyed the city and very many people were killed, and more captives taken. But I know the exiles will go home at last and build the city again and rebuild the Temple and give it back to God.

This is what the Lord God says: "I mean to go looking for this flock of mine, search for it myself, as a shepherd goes looking for his scattered sheep. I will rescue them from all the dark places into which they have strayed in the mist. I will find them and bring them home again; they shall have a true shepherd at last."

And he showed me this vision, too, to cheer them. It seemed that I was carried away by the spirit of God and set down in the middle of a great plain. The whole of this plain was covered thick with the bones of men, all old and dry. It looked as if a great battle had been fought there long ago, and the dead left unburied. "Son of man," said the Voice of God, "can these bones live?"

"Lord God," I said, "only You know."

Then he told me to speak aloud, prophesying to these dry bones, and I said, "Listen, dry bones, to a message from the Lord God. He says: 'I mean to send my spirit into you and restore you to life. Sinews shall join you again, flesh grow upon you, and skin cover you, and I will give you the breath of life. Will you doubt then the Lord's power?' "

As I was speaking, a sound came and a great stirring all over the plain. The bones came together, each to its own joint. And as I watched, I saw the flesh clothe them and the skin cover them, but they still lay dead upon the plain.

"Son of man," said the Voice of God, "give this message to the breath of life, from the Lord God: 'Come, breath of life, from the four winds, and breathe upon these slain to make them live.' " So I prophesied as He told me, and the breath of life came into them, and they stood up, a great army, host upon host of them.

"See," said the Voice of God. "These bones are the whole race of Israel. They are complaining that all hope is lost to them. It is for you to give them this message from me: 'I mean to bring you back from your graves and give you life again, my people. I mean to bring you home to your own land. Will you doubt me then? What I promise, I do.' "

⌒

Isaiah's Story

Isaiah was a great prophet who lived in Jerusalem about a hundred fifty years before Ezekiel was born. He prophesied more about our Lord than anyone else and was altogether a wonderful person. He had one vision of angels that we remember every time we go to Mass. They were rather like Ezekiel's angels, but he called them seraphim instead of cherubim. This is how he tells about it:

In the year when King Ozias died, I had a vision. I saw the Lord sitting on a throne that towered high above me. The skirts of His robe filled the Temple, and above it rose the seraphim. Each of them had six wings. With two of their wings they hid the face of God, with two His feet, and with the other two they flew. And as they flew, they cried aloud, "Holy, holy, holy, Lord God of armies; all the earth is full of His glory."

The lintels over the Temple doors rang with the sound of their voices, and smoke went up, filling the Temple courts.

"Alas," said I, "that I dare not speak. I am all dirty with sin, and so is everyone in this whole country. My lips are not clean enough to speak to God, even though my eyes have seen my king, the Lord of Armies."

Then one of the seraphim took a pair of tongs and with it picked up a burning coal from the altar. With this he flew to me and touched my mouth.

"Now that this has touched your lips," he said, "your guilt is all swept away; you are forgiven."

And I heard the Lord say, "Who shall be my messenger? Who is to go on this errand of ours?"

And I said, "I am here at Your command. Make me Your messenger."

That is why, before he reads the Gospel at Mass, the priest prays that God will clean his lips as He cleaned the lips of the prophet Isaiah, with a burning coal. And like the seraphim, we sing, "Holy, holy, holy" at Mass before the eucharistic prayer.

Chapter Eight

Job and His Friends

When this story was written, long before our Lord came, no one knew very much about life after death. They thought this life was the one that mattered. So if a man was good, they expected God to reward him by giving him everything he wanted in this world. And if a man was bad, they expected God to punish him right away. Of course, God didn't do that then any more than He does now.

The man who wrote the story of Job had thought a great deal about this and puzzled over it. He was a poet, so at last he wrote a whole long story about it, all in verse. At the beginning he put a conversation between God and the Devil to show how God happened to be so hard on Job. Of course, the Devil doesn't really go up to Heaven and stand among the angels, chatting with God. But poets are allowed to invent things like that.

The land of Hus was northeast of Palestine. This story was written a long time after the Israelites came back to the Promised Land, but the poet wrote his poem about a much earlier time, as people now make up stories about the Indians and cowboys who lived a hundred years ago. Some of these stories are made up about real people, and it is most likely there really was a great and patient man called Job who lived about the time of Abraham.

There are no Israelites in this story, because the man who wrote it wanted to show that God cares about other people besides His chosen ones. At least, people think that is why; we can't really be sure, of course.

This is the story:

There was a man in the land of Hus whose name was Job. He was a good, honest man, and a rich one, too. Although he was not a Jew, he worshiped the true God and had no use for idols. Job and his wife had ten children, seven sons and three daughters. For wealth, he had seven thousand sheep, three thousand camels, a thousand oxen, five hundred donkeys, and as many servants as ever he needed to look after all these animals and his own family and house and garden, too.

No one in all the East was more respected than Job, because he was so rich and so good. His seven sons lived in houses of their own, and they took turns giving parties. To these each one in turn invited all his brothers and their three sisters, too. Job used to offer a burnt sacrifice for all his children every morning and always prayed hard that God would forgive them if they had done anything wrong.

One day, when the angels were standing before God in Heaven, the One Who Is Against Us was there among them.

"Where have you been?" God said to him.

"Walking about the earth," said the One Who Is Against Us. "To and fro, to and fro."

"Why, then," said God, "you must have seen my servant Job. What a good man he is! What an honest man; he does nothing wrong."

"Job obeys You," said the One Who Is Against Us, "and it pays him well. You protect him from all harm. No troubles come to Job; he and his family and all his riches are safe in Your care. But if You took his wealth away, how quickly he would turn against You!"

"Do you think so?" said God. "Very well. We will see. I give you leave to do what you please with everything that belongs to him. Only you must not hurt Job himself."

The One Who Is Against Us was well satisfied with that and went down to the earth again.

And that same day, a messenger came to Job and said, "Your oxen were plowing and your donkeys were grazing nearby. Suddenly a band of robbers swept down on them. They killed the plowmen and the boys who were minding the donkeys and drove all the oxen and donkeys away. And I alone escaped to tell the tale."

While he was still speaking, another messenger came in. "Lightning struck your sheep," he said. "They were all killed, and so were the shepherds. And I alone escaped to tell the tale."

Close on his heels came a third messenger, who said, "Three bands of robbers have killed the men who were tending your camels, and they drove the camels off with them. And I alone escaped to tell the tale."

Just behind him came a fourth messenger, who said, "I have come from the party your eldest son was giving in his house. Your other sons and daughters were there. All of a sudden, a great wind from across the desert struck the house, and it fell. All who were in it were killed. And I alone escaped to tell the tale."

Job stood up and tore his clothes to show how shocked he was and then he made this prayer to God: "I brought nothing with me into this world, and I shall take nothing with me when I leave it. The Lord gave me riches and children, and the Lord has taken them away. None of this could have happened if it were not His will. Blessed be the name of the Lord!"

Next time the angels stood before God, with the One Who Is Against Us among them, God said to him, "Where have you been?"

"To and fro, to and fro on the earth," said the One Who Is Against Us.

"Why, then," said God, "you have seen for yourself that there never was a man so good as my servant Job. He fears me and never does wrong. In spite of all you have done to him, he is still as good as gold. It is a shame that he has been so ill treated, and all for nothing."

"Ah!" said the One Who Is Against Us, "but You have only taken away what belonged to him. Hurt the man himself, and see if he does not turn against You then!"

"Very well," said God. "You have my leave to do what you please with him. Only leave him alive."

With that, the One Who Is Against Us went down to earth and took Job's health from him. He gave him a terrible itchy disease. Poor Job went and sat on the rubbish heap in his garden and scratched himself with a broken plate; he was so very itchy and miserable. Even his wife turned on him. "Are you still trying to be good?" she said. "What use has it been to you? You might as well lose your faith in God and kill yourself."

"Spoken like a foolish wife," said Job. "Should we accept the good things God sends us and not the bad?"

Of all Job's friends, only three came to comfort him, and these three came from far away. Their names were Eliphaz, Bildad, and Zophar. When they first saw Job, they hardly knew him. But when they understood that the miserable man sitting on the rubbish heap scratching himself was really Job, they tore their clothes, threw dust in the air, and wept aloud. It sounds like odd behavior for people visiting an invalid, but it was perfectly polite in those days.

Then, for a whole week, they sat on the ground beside Job without saying anything. They could see he felt terrible. At last, Job broke the silence, which must have been getting rather trying. "I wish," said Job, "that I had never been born."

Eliphaz answered him, "Do not take what I say amiss, but you used to be so good at comforting other people in their troubles and telling them about the goodness of God. Now that the trouble is your own, you seem rather upset. And you know as well as we do that God never allows such things to happen to an innocent man. God never punishes a man without reason, does He?" And he said a great deal more.

"If God would only finish what He has begun and kill me," said poor Job, "I would be quite content. You were kind to come to visit me, but now I can see you wish you had stayed at home! But as you are here, tell me, what have I done that God should treat me like this?" And he said a great deal more.

Then said Bildad, "Are you still complaining? If you have really done nothing wrong, no doubt God will hear you as soon as you turn to Him. If you are innocent, you have only to pray, and you will get well again!" And he said a great deal more.

"How could I defend myself to God?" said Job. "I can only ask for mercy, even though I am in the right." And he said a great deal more.

Zophar came in, in his turn. "You have plenty to say," he said to Job, "so you ought to be willing to listen. All your talk will not make you innocent. You must have done something terrible to be punished so by God." And that was not all he said.

"Nonsense!" said Job. "Do you think there are no wicked men who have grown rich by robbery, and who enjoy their wealth all their lives? And yet I know that

God knows all things and deals with every man just as He pleases." And he said a great deal more.

"Now I see plainly that you are guilty," said Eliphaz. "Everyone knows that God punishes the wicked and rewards the good. There are a thousand stories to prove it."

"Old tales and cold comfort," said Job to his friends, and to God he said, "If only You would come to my help, I would not care who else was against me!"

After that, it was Bildad's turn again, and so it went on. The length of the conversation Job's three comforters had with him when they did get started quite made up for the week spent in silence when they arrived. But it always came back to the same thing: the three friends said Job must be wicked or he would not be in such a miserable state, and Job said he had done no wrong. After a time, he was saying it rather sharply, and you can't blame him.

When everybody had had their say several times over, they were all silent at last. Then up jumped a young man called Elihu, who had been listening to all the talk.

"I can see," said he, "that although you are all much older than I am, you are not at all wise. Job complains of God as though He were another man and must answer to us for what He does. But it is God who has the whole world in His care. We have no life, no breath, no hope unless He gives it to us. He made everything — or did you help Him, Job? His power and majesty are such that no one of us can give Him enough praise, and none of us has a right to complain of the way He treats us."

So said Elihu, and Job said nothing, so all four of them went home and left Job. And then a storm came up and a whirlwind, and out of the whirlwind, Job heard the voice of God Himself speaking.

"It is my turn to ask questions," said the Voice. "Do you think you are able to judge what I do? Was it you who made the world? When I made the morning stars and they all sang together for joy, were you there? Was it you or I who locked the sea between the countries of the earth? Can you tell the day when to dawn? Have you seen the dark depths of the ocean? Do you know what world lies beyond the gates of death? Did you foresee the day you would be born, and do you know how many years you have left to live? Can you command the cold that turns water hard as stone? And which of us feeds the wild animals, in the desert? To which of us do the baby lions and the young birds cry for food?"

And Job said, "I am listening with my finger on my lips. I will not say a word. I have spoken foolishly, and I wish that I had said nothing at all. Only you know what is to come, and I will do penance for questioning Your ways."

Then the Voice of God was heard by Eliphaz, the eldest of Job's three comforters: "I am angry with you and your two friends," said the Voice. "Job never displeased me or spoke so foolishly of me as you have. Go to him, all three of you, with seven bulls and seven rams to offer in sacrifice. Only Job's prayers will save you. He was innocent and spoke truly of me, and you did not."

So the three friends came to Job again, with seven bulls and seven rams, and very foolish they must have looked. But Job, who was perfectly well again, prayed for them, and they offered the bulls and rams to God in sacrifice, and God forgave them. What's more, all Job's other friends who had stayed away from him all this time, heard that God was on his side after all. Then they came to him with large and handsome gifts and said they were so sorry for all his troubles; they had just happened to hear about them. . . .

They brought him so many presents and things went so well with him after that, that he was soon richer than he had ever been. And he had seven more sons and three more daughters. These three daughters were the prettiest girls anyone had ever seen. Their names were Fair as Day, Sweet as Cassia, and Dark Eyelids.

Job lived so long that he was a great-great-grandfather before he died.

And now you know what people mean when they talk about "Job's comforters."

Chapter Nine

When Our Lord Came

All the stories of angels in this book so far have been about the time before our Lord was born.

Ever since Adam and Eve sinned and were sorry, all the history of the world had looked forward to His coming. Abraham was the first to hear a hint of it, and he did not understand in what way the people descended from him were to bring a blessing on all the nations of the world. He knew only that somehow it would be so.

When his grandson Jacob was dying, he gave a blessing to each of his twelve sons. When it was his son Judah's turn, Jacob said, "There will always be a prince of Judah's family until he who is to be sent to us comes, the hope of all nations." Judah is one of the ancestors of our Lord, so it is easy for us to see what he meant, although it may well have puzzled Judah.

All through the long history of God's Chosen People, He was teaching them slowly to understand Him better: how to worship Him, how to be faithful to Him, and more about that Someone who was to come. God taught the Jews, His Chosen People, as He does us, by means of

109

men. Moses was their first great teacher. He gave them
the Ten Commandments and a law to live by. That was
while they were in the desert, after they had been so long
in Egypt. After they came home to the Promised Land,
God gave them judges to rule them in His name and to
teach them about Him. The last of these was Samuel,
who was a great man and a prophet as well as a judge. He
was sent by God to choose their first two kings for them.

The second of these kings was David, the best and
greatest of all their kings. He really tried to please God,
and did, and he never worshiped idols or prayed to any
god but the true God. He wrote a lot of the prayers we
call psalms. David's son, Solomon, who built God's Temple in Jerusalem, although he started so well, fell into
idolatry in his old age. It came of having a great many
foreign wives who worshiped idols and persuaded Solomon to worship them, too.

Some of the kings who came after this were fairly
good and some of them quite bad, and none of them very
great. In the meantime, God kept sending prophets to
bring people back to Him when they had taken to worshiping idols. The prophets also taught them what they
must do to please God, and what would happen to them
if they went on disobeying Him. The prophets told them
more about the One who was to come, too: He was to be
born in Bethlehem, and He was to be a descendant of
David. He would rule His people gloriously forever and
conquer all the nations of the world. There were other

prophecies that said He would suffer for their sins, and be poor and ill-treated. They did not understand how that could be, so they thought mostly about the prophecies of a great king who would make their country the most important and grandest in the world. And we would have done just the same.

Three of these prophets are in this book: Daniel, Isaiah, and Ezekiel. The Israelites sometimes listened to their prophets and did as they were told, and then all went well. But much more often, they refused to listen and thought they could manage their own affairs better than God could. And when that happened, everything went very badly. But all the same, they did get to know more about God as time went on.

And at last, it was almost time for this great king to come. They called him the Messiah, which means "the Anointed." All their kings were anointed when they were chosen to rule, but this one was to be God's Anointed and chosen King in a special way; some of the prophecies about Him called Him the Son of God, and some called Him the Son of Man. But no one understood then that He would really be God and man, too. No one knew that before our Lord's coming.

Before He came, just before, came the last of the prophets: His cousin, John the Baptist. Of course you know the story of his birth and the story of how our Lord came into the world, but they are in this book: they are stories no one can hear too often, and they are full of angels, too.

⌐

Gabriel and Zachary

Zachary was one of the priests of the Temple in Jerusalem. There were far more priests than were needed, so they used to take turns; each served for a week at a time and then went home until his turn came around again. Zachary's home was in a little village out in the country, about five miles from Jerusalem. He had a wife called Elizabeth, and they were both as good as gold and very happy — except for one thing. Like Abraham's wife, Sara, Elizabeth had never had a baby, even though she and Zachary had both prayed and prayed for one. And now they were both so old they had given up all hope that their prayers would be heard.

Offering incense in the Temple was such a special thing to do that no priest was allowed to do it more than once in his whole life. The one who was to do it was chosen from all the priests who had not yet had their turn. They drew lots for it. Zachary had drawn lots so often, hoping it would be his turn — and at last it was!

So he was very pleased and happy when he went into the sanctuary of the Temple to offer incense. No one could see into the sanctuary; everyone else stayed outside and said their prayers, waiting for him to come out and tell them the incense was offered.

As Zachary stood by the altar, spreading incense on hot coals, he suddenly saw an angel standing beside the altar.

He was very frightened, but the angel said, "Do not be afraid, Zachary. Your prayers have been heard. Elizabeth is to have a baby, and you are to call him John. He will bring great joy to you and to many other people as well, for he is to prepare for the coming of the Lord, making His people ready to receive Him."

If Zachary had only remembered about Abraham and Sarah and how they had a baby when they were old! But he didn't. He said, "Give me a sign that this is true. We are old, Elizabeth and I."

Then the angel did give him cause to be frightened. He said, "I am Gabriel, one of the angels who stand in the presence of God. He sent me to bring you this good news. Because you have not believed me, you will not be able to speak until after the child is born." Then Gabriel vanished, and sure enough, Zachary found he couldn't say a word.

Meanwhile, those who were waiting for him to come back from offering incense wondered why he was taking so long. When he appeared, he couldn't tell them; he could only make signs. He made them understand that he had seen a vision, and they went away wondering about it.

Zachary went home to Elizabeth, and sure enough, she presently found she was going to have a baby.

Gabriel and Our Lady

Six months after this, Gabriel was sent on another errand, the loveliest any angel ever had. This time he went to a little town far away from Jerusalem, up in the hills of Galilee. It was early spring when he went there, so the hills were covered with fresh green grass and so many wildflowers you could hardly walk without treading on them.

Gabriel went into one of the little houses in the town where a girl called Mary lived. She was engaged to a carpenter whose name was Joseph.

When he saw her, Gabriel said, "Hail, full of grace, the Lord is with you. Blessed are you among women."

People who see angels are usually frightened, but Mary was only puzzled. What could an angel mean by greeting her like that? But Gabriel, who was used to everybody being frightened of him, said, "Mary, do not be afraid. God loves you very much. You are going to have a baby, and you are to call Him Jesus. The Lord God will give Him the throne of His father David, and He shall reign forever. His kingdom will never have an end."

Mary said, "How is this to be done?"

The angel answered, "The Holy Spirit will come upon you, and your baby will be the Son of God. Your cousin Elizabeth is going to have a baby, too, old as she is, because nothing is impossible for God."

Mary said, "Behold the handmaid of the Lord. Let it happen to me just as you say."

Then Gabriel went back to Heaven, and our Lady went to visit her dear cousin Elizabeth. She stayed with her until her baby, little St. John the Baptist, was born, and then she came home to Nazareth and married Joseph the carpenter.

She did not tell him about Gabriel or about the baby she was to have, because it was a secret. She knew God would let Joseph know about it, and so He did. He sent an angel with the message, and the angel gave it to Joseph while he was asleep. All the angels who came with messages to St. Joseph came when he was asleep; he dreamed them, but they were true dreams, sent by God. He always did just as the angels had told him.

When it was nearly time for our Lady's baby to be born, she and Joseph heard that the government was taking a census, as governments still do. They wanted to count how many people were living in the whole country. For this census, everyone had to go back to the town his family had come from and be counted. Joseph's hometown was Bethlehem, not Nazareth, so they had to go there to put in their names.

It was quite a long journey from Nazareth to Bethlehem. The only way of getting there was to walk or to ride horses or donkeys. Horses were only for rich people, but most likely our Lady and St. Joseph had a donkey. So she would have ridden, and St. Joseph would have walked along beside her. They traveled like this for about four days, camping at night, or staying in one of the inns by the roadside. When they got to Bethlehem at last, they found the little town overflowing; there were so many people who had to put in their names there.

The inn was full, and no one had a room for them. But someone told them of a cave that was used as a stable; there they could get out of the cold wind and have soft hay to sleep on. So they went very thankfully into this little cave, and there, as everyone knows, the baby Jesus was born. Our Lady wrapped her Baby in bands of linen, called swaddling clothes, and put Him in the manger for a cradle.

The very first people to hear about our Lord's birth were shepherds camping in the fields outside Bethlehem. There was good grass there for their sheep, but there were wolves, too. It wasn't safe to leave the sheep alone at night. So the shepherds took turns sitting up and keeping watch until morning.

In the middle of the night, these shepherds suddenly saw an angel standing beside them and the glory of God shining over everything. They were terrified, but the angel said, "Do not be afraid! This day a Savior is born to you, the Lord Christ Himself. You will know Him, because He is wrapped in swaddling clothes and lying in a manger."

All of a sudden, the shepherds saw crowds and crowds of angels, all the armies of Heaven, standing with the first angel and praising God, saying: "Glory to God in the highest, and peace to men of goodwill!"

Mary and Joseph were still in Bethlehem when the wise men from the East, whom we know as the Three Kings, came to adore our Lord. They went to King Herod in Jerusalem and asked him, "Where shall we find the baby who is born King of the Jews? We saw His star in the East and have come to adore Him."

Herod, who was reigning as king of Jerusalem, was not a Jew and had no right to the throne. He had gotten it by war and trickery and by making friends with the Romans. So he was not at all pleased to hear this, nor were those who liked him being king. He called together all the most learned people in his kingdom and asked them, "Where is the Christ to be born?"

"In Bethlehem," they told him. "One of the prophets said He would be born there."

Then Herod called the wise men to him and asked them how long ago they had seen this star and how long they had been on their journey. When they told him, he sent them on their way to Bethlehem, saying, "When you have found this Child, come back and tell me, so that I can go and adore Him, too."

When the wise men reached Bethlehem, they saw the same star they had seen in their own country. It went in front of them, guiding them to the house where Mary and Joseph and the Baby were living. And when it reached the house, it stood still.

The wise men were happy beyond words at seeing this. They went into the house and found the Baby there, with His Mother, Mary. When they had adored Him, they gave Him the gifts they had brought, gold and frankincense and myrrh.

That night, God warned the wise men in their sleep not to trust Herod, but to start back to their own country by a road that went nowhere near Jerusalem.

As soon as they had gone, an angel came to Joseph in a dream. "Get up at once," the angel said to him, "and take the Child and His Mother away. You must go to Egypt, and quickly, for Herod will be looking for the Child to kill Him."

So Joseph got up and woke our Lady, and they got the donkey ready and started for Egypt right away.

When Herod heard that the wise men had gone home without coming back to tell him where the Baby was, he was furious. He thought he would make himself safe anyway; he sent his soldiers to kill all the boy babies in Bethlehem who were not yet two years old. And they did. It was all right for the babies; they were some of the first people to get to Heaven. But it was terrible for their mothers and fathers.

When that was done, Herod felt quite safe. He knew very little about God and nothing about angels! And anyway, it was only a short time after this that he died. An angel came to Egypt to tell St. Joseph about it. "You can go back now," he said. "The people who wanted to kill the Child are dead."

They set out to come back to Bethlehem, where St. Joseph seems to have wanted to make their home, instead of Nazareth. But on the way, he heard that one of Herod's sons, who was nearly as nasty as his father, was the new king. St. Joseph was warned in a dream that he should go to Nazareth, not Bethlehem. Bethlehem was only a few miles from Jerusalem. Nazareth, far away in the hill country, was much safer.

Chapter Ten

Our Lord and the Angels

The next story about an angel in the Gospels is about a fallen angel.

After our Lord grew up, He went on being a carpenter until He was about thirty years old. Then He left Nazareth because He knew it was time for Him to begin the work He had come into the world to do. To prepare for it, He went into the desert to fast and pray. He was all alone except for the animals that lived there, and He had nothing to eat. When He had been there for forty days, He was very hungry.

Now, the Devil had never been able to make out why he didn't seem to be able to get any hold on our Lord. He did not know that He was God, but he knew there was something extraordinary about Him, something the Devil couldn't understand. Perhaps He was the Messiah, the Great King who the prophets said would come. That is what the Devil meant by "the Son of God."

Now he saw how weak our Lord was from His long fast, and he thought, "This is just the time to get the better of Him!"

He came up to our Lord and said, "If You are the Son of God, tell these stones to turn into loaves of bread." But our Lord said, "Men do not live only by eating bread; all the words of God bring them life, too."

The Devil, seeing that was no use, took our Lord up to the tip of the highest pinnacle of the Temple. "If You are the Son of God," he said, "throw Yourself down. It is written in the holy Scriptures that He has given His angels charge of You, and they will hold You up in their hands in case you should hurt Your foot on a stone."

"But it is also written," said our Lord, "that you shall not put the Lord your God to the proof." He meant that it is wrong to ask God for a miracle just to see whether He can do it.

The Devil tried again. He took our Lord up to the top of a high mountain and showed Him all the kingdoms of the world, and how rich and glorious they were. "All these I will give You," the Devil said, "if You fall down and adore me."

This must have seemed to the good angels as ridiculous as anything they had ever heard. Our Lord had made the whole world, and here was the Devil kindly offering to give Him a piece of it!

Our Lord said, "Away with you, Satan. It is written in the Scriptures, 'You shall worship the Lord your God and serve none but Him.' "

Then the Devil left Him, and good angels came and brought Him food and all He needed.

There are no more good angels in the Gospels for a long time after that, but plenty of bad ones, far too many to put in this book.

In those days, it often happened that the Devil took possession of somebody. Then, sometimes, the man who was possessed could not say or do what he wanted to, but only what the Devil made him do. It was a very frightening thing, and it still happens now and again, but usually in countries where very few people are baptized. The Devil has more power in places where people know nothing about our Lord, but still he hasn't nearly so much power as he had before our Lord died for us. Nothing of the sort can happen to you or me unless we decide to be as wicked as we possibly can, and it isn't very likely even then.

All through the three years when our Lord was teaching His Apostles and preaching to crowds and healing the sick, people were brought to Him who were possessed by the Devil. Here is one of the most surprising stories about a possessed man.

The Devils Who Wouldn't Go Home

One evening, our Lord and His Apostles sailed across the sea from Galilee to the opposite shore. Some of the people who had been listening to Him preach decided to go, too; they got into any boat that would take them and sailed after Him.

The place where they landed on the opposite coast was very wild and rocky. There was a precipice on one side and, above that, rolling country going up to a mountain. On the other side was a graveyard. There were tombs like little caves cut into the rocks, some of them sealed up and some empty and open. Between the precipice and the mountain there was a great herd of pigs — two thousand of them — with swineherds looking after them.

It looked at first as if the swineherds were the only people there, but when our Lord and His Apostles had landed, they heard a shout, and a most extraordinary-looking man came from among the tombs and ran up to our Lord. His hair and beard were wild and matted; there was blood on his body, and he wore no clothes at all. This weird-looking creature fell down at our Lord's feet and cried out, "Why do you interfere with me, Jesus, Son of the Most High God?"

He was a man the Devil had taken possession of, and it was the Devil who spoke through his mouth. Time and again, this man had been bound and chained up as a dangerous madman, but the Devil always broke the chains and drove him out into wild, lonely places. No one had tried to chain him for a long time now; he lived among the tombs, crying out and cutting himself with sharp stones.

Our Lord said, speaking to the devil in this miserable creature, "What is your name?"

And He got the very odd answer: "Legion." There was not just one devil in the man, but a whole division, several regiments of them!

"Come out of him," said our Lord.

But the devils clamored and implored, "Do not send us back to Hell! Please do not send us back to Hell! Instead, let us go into those pigs."

The Devil is all for us going to Hell, but he will do anything at all to stay away from it himself.

Our Lord gave the devils leave to go into the pigs, and the whole herd rushed straight for the edge of the cliff and went over it into the sea. The swineherds were so frightened, they took to their heels and made off as fast as they could. They went to the pigs' owners to tell what had happened and, on their way, told everybody they met.

Presently a little crowd of people arrived to see what on earth was going on. They found near the shore our Lord and the Apostles and the people who had crossed the sea with them. And sitting on the ground by our Lord's feet was the man who had been possessed by the devils and whom they knew as a dangerous madman. But now he was dressed, clean and tidy, and perfectly sensible. To see this frightened them even more than hearing what had happened to the pigs. All they could think of to do was to ask our Lord to please go away.

So He and the Apostles went back to their boat and sailed across the sea again. The man who had been possessed wanted to go with our Lord, but He wouldn't allow it. He said what the man must do was to go home and tell everybody what God had done for him. So he did that faithfully, and no doubt went happily to Heaven when he died.

This is rather a frightening story, but no one who loves our Lord need ever be frightened of the Devil. Our guardian angels are always ready to send him off whenever we ask them to. We have our Lord's own word for it that every child has a guardian angel. He said, "They have angels of their own in Heaven who see the face of my heavenly Father continually."

The Garden of Gethsemane

The next good angel in the Gospels is a very sad one: the angel who came to comfort our Lord in the Garden of Gethsemane, on the night when He was betrayed by Judas to His enemies. That was the night, you remember, when our Lord prayed and prayed and asked Peter, James, and John to stay awake and pray, too. But they kept going to sleep; they just couldn't seem to keep awake.

But they woke up when the crowd of people, with Judas among them, came to arrest our Lord. That was when Peter pulled out a sword he had and cut off the right ear of one of the high priest's servants! And he would have struck again, but our Lord said, "Put away your sword! Those who kill with swords are killed by them. Don't you know that I have only to ask my Father, even now, and

He will send me more than twelve legions of angels right away? But if I asked for them, how would the prophecies about my death be fulfilled?"

Then He turned to the men who were holding Him, and said, "Just let me do this," and put out His hand and touched the ear Peter had cut off, and it was firm in its place again, as good as new.

"You have come to arrest me with swords and clubs," He said, "as if I were a thief. But when I used to sit every day teaching in the Temple, you never laid hands on me."

Then the Apostles all ran off and left Him, and He let the soldiers lead Him away to die for us.

But when you hear someone say, "Why does God allow so many good Christians to be killed?" "Why does God allow so much power to wicked men?" "Why does God allow war?" and so on, it's worth remembering that our Lord can have more than twelve legions of angels any time, just by asking for them. Twelve legions is about seventy-two thousand angels! Much more use, surely, than twelve frightened Apostles! And very much more use than all of us whom He uses to do His work in this world now. If He still doesn't ask for them, there must be some very good reason, even if we can't see what it is. But we shall see Him leading His legions of angels at the end of the world.

Chapter Eleven

The Most Joyful Angels of All

In our Lord's country, people used to bury their dead in tombs cut like little caves in the rocky sides of hills. They kept the entrances small and hollowed out a little room inside, with a shelf of rock to put the body on. The entrance was closed by rolling a big, round, flat stone up against it.

That was the sort of tomb Joseph of Arimathea had had made for himself. It was all ready for him whenever he should die, but on Good Friday evening, he took our Lord's body and put it there instead. It was in a garden, quite close to where our Lord was crucified. Our Lady and Mary Magdalen and James's mother, who was called Mary too, helped him.

Joseph had fine new linen to wrap our Lord's body in, and sweet spices and herbs to anoint it with, but it was the evening before the Sabbath day, and they had to do everything in too much of a hurry. The Sabbath day, Saturday, the last day of the week, was a day of rest on which no work at all was allowed to be done. So Mary Magdalen and James's mother planned to come back and

129

finish anointing our Lord's body first thing on Sunday morning.

Very early on Sunday, before it was even light, they set out for the tomb. Perhaps they wondered why our Lady didn't go with them, or perhaps they thought she was too sad to come. But we know why she didn't go.

As they walked along, it began to get light, and they hurried. One thing bothered them. What were they to do about the great stone closing the tomb? They knew it was much too big and heavy for them to move, and they wondered whom they could get to help them move it.

Then they reached the garden and saw the tomb, with — oh, dear! — soldiers standing on guard in front of it. And then all at once, things began to happen. There was an earthquake, and they saw an angel rolling back the stone, and when he had rolled it back, he sat on it. His face was so bright, it made them think of lightning, and his clothes were shining white, like snow. The soldiers were so frightened, they fainted!

The angel took no notice of them, but spoke to the two Marys. "Do not be afraid," he said. "I know you are looking for Jesus, who was crucified. But He has risen, as He said He would. Come and see the place where His body lay."

The women went into the tomb and found two more angels there, like young men in shining clothes. And sure enough, our Lord's body was nowhere to be seen.

"Why are you looking for a living man among the dead?" said one of the angels. "He is not here; He is risen.

Don't you remember what He said to you in Galilee? 'The Son of Man must be delivered into the hands of sinful men and be crucified, but on the third day He will rise again.' Go and tell His disciples and Peter that He will go ahead of you to Galilee. You will see Him there, as He promised."

That was how the news was first given that death had no hold on our Lord. Since God first made the world, there have never been angels with such a joyful message.

After our Lord's Resurrection, He stayed in the world for forty days. At the end of that time, He took His Apostles for a last walk. They went out through the valley east of Jerusalem, over the little brook called Kidron, the same way He had gone to the Garden of Gethsemane. But this time they went on, past the garden, and out to the village of Bethany, so that our Lord could say good-bye to His friends there. Then they climbed to the top of Mount Olivet, and there our Lord lifted up His hands and blessed them, and as He did it, He rose up into the air. They watched Him going up, until two white-robed angels came and stood beside them.

"Why do you stand there, looking up to Heaven?" they said. "Jesus will come back again, in the same way as you have seen Him go."

And so He will, but there was work for the Apostles to do first, just as there is for us.

Chapter Twelve

The Apostles and the Angels

After Pentecost, the Apostles' first adventure with an angel happened like this: it was before they had left Jerusalem, while they were still converting as many as they could of the people who lived there. They all used to go to the part of the Temple called Solomon's Porch and there tell whoever wanted to hear all about our Lord.

All the way along the street leading to the Temple, sick people and cripples used to wait for the Apostles to come, because our Lord had given them power to cure people, just as He used to. It was discovered presently that if Peter's shadow fell on one of these sick people, he was cured at once, so after that, no doubt, the sick people were thickest on the side where his shadow would fall!

All this made the high priest and the people who had plotted our Lord's death furious. They had thought they were finished with Him when He was crucified, and now here were His followers stirring everything up again. They were so angry, they arrested all the Apostles and put them in prison. It was too late to try them that day, so they left them in prison for the night. In the morning, they called the council together with all the grandest people in Jerusalem in attendance. When they were quite ready, they sent to the prison to have the Apostles brought in.

And then there was a fine to-do! Not one apostle could the prison guards find in all the prison. After they had looked in every possible and impossible place, they came back to the council and said, "We found the prison locked up with all proper care, and the guards at their posts in front of the door. But when we unlocked it, there was no one there!"

What had happened? And where in the world were the Apostles? No one could imagine, until someone strolled in and said, "Did you know that those men you arrested last night are back in Solomon's Porch, preaching again?"

It was very simple really, although the council could never understand it. God didn't want the Apostles to be kept in prison just then, so He had sent an angel to let them out during the night. The angel had given them a message, too. "Go and take your stand in the Temple," he said, "and preach the words of life as usual."

So as soon as the Temple gates were opened in the morning, that was just what the Apostles had done.

⌒

Cornelius and the Angel

In the first years of our Lord's Church, everybody in it was Jewish. Our Lord had told the Apostles to preach the gospel to all the nations of the world, so they knew that, in the end, non-Jews were to be preached to also, after His own people were converted.

It never occurred to the Apostles that these people would not have to learn to be good Jews as well as good Christians. They didn't understand that the old rules of the law, under which they had grown up, were no longer binding. The rules had been given them as part of God's religion for His Chosen People. It took a miracle to make them understand that they did not matter anymore.

What sort of rules were they, and why were they given? When the Chosen People first came to the Promised Land and for a long time afterward, the people who lived around them had quite horrible religions. They worshiped idols in all kinds of silly and nasty ways. The Devil was behind it, of course.

The extraordinary thing is that God's people, who had a religion given to them by Him, were always longing to go off and worship idols, too. It sounds quite mad to us, but idols were the fashion in those days; everybody else had idols, and not having any made the Israelites feel out of it. So every time they made friends with people outside their race, they made friends with their idols, too. They were always having to be told that they must not do this.

One idea they had learned, and really understood, was that sin is like dirt. So the best way to make them understand the wickedness of pagan religions was to tell them that these religions were dirty. And they were told so again and again. Their own religion was clean and made them clean; pagan religions were unclean and made those who belonged to them unclean, too. And some animals were unclean as well, they were taught, and not fit for them to eat. These were mostly things like snakes and lizards and birds that live on carrion, which it's hard to imagine anyone wanting to eat. They were forbidden to eat pigs, too, which we do eat, but it is still not a good idea to eat pork in a hot country where there are no refrigerators.

The Jews had quite gotten over wanting idols by the time our Lord came, but they still kept the old rules about having as little to do with non-Jews as possible, and they still obeyed the laws about what they must not eat.

But you can see that something very special had to happen to make them understand that the new Kingdom of God really was for everybody.

This is what happened:

There was a Roman officer called Cornelius stationed at Caesarea, which is a town by the sea in Palestine. He had a house there and lots of friends, for he was a very nice man and a very good one, too. Although he was not a Jew, he was quite sure the God of the Jews was the true God, and he prayed to Him every day. He gave all the money he could to the poor Jews who lived in Caesarea; he was really trying to be good.

Well, one afternoon, about three o'clock, Cornelius was in his room saying some afternoon prayers, and suddenly an angel came into his room and said, "Cornelius!"

Cornelius looked at him in terror and said, "What is it, Lord?"

"Your prayers and almsgiving are not forgotten by God," said the angel. "And now He wants you to send men to Joppa to bring here a man called Peter. He is lodging with a tanner called Simon, whose house is close to the sea. He will tell you what God wants you to do."

With that, the angel left him. Cornelius called two of his servants and one of the soldiers under him who he knew worshiped God as he did. He told them about the angel and sent them off to Joppa to find Peter. The angel was right, of course: Peter was in Joppa. He had gone there to visit some new Christians.

Next day, while Cornelius's servants were on their way, Peter went up on the roof of Simon's house. Most of the houses there have flat roofs, and people use them as we do a porch, as a sort of extra room when the weather is warm and dry. Peter was trying to say his prayers up on the roof, but he was very hungry and kept hoping dinner would be ready soon. Perhaps he could smell it cooking.

While he was up there, he fell into a trance. In his trance, he saw the skies open and a great bundle like a sheet coming down from the sky. It looked as if someone up there was holding it by its four corners and letting the middle part down to the earth. When it was low enough for Peter to see into it, he saw that it was full of all kinds of creatures, animals and creeping things and birds, and many of them were of kinds that counted as "unclean."

As he was looking at this sort of zoo in a sheet, he heard a voice say, "Get up, Peter. Kill some of these, and eat them."

But Peter, looking at all the horrid crawly things in the sheet, said, "I cannot, Lord. Never in my life have I eaten anything unclean."

"It is not for you to call anything unclean that God has made clean," the voice said.

All this happened three times, and then the sheet was drawn up through the sky again. Peter was as puzzled as could be; he couldn't imagine why he should have been shown such an odd vision.

But while he was still wondering about it, he heard the Holy Spirit say to him, "There are three men asking for you downstairs; go down to them, and go with them as they ask you. You need not have any doubts about it; it is I who have sent them to you."

Peter went down from the roof, and, sure enough, there were Cornelius's messengers asking for him.

"Here I am," he said. "What is it you want of me?"

"The centurion Cornelius," they said, "has had a vision of one of God's holy angels. The angel told him to send messengers to bring you to his house; he is waiting there to hear all you have to tell him."

Peter knew that a Roman officer with an Italian name was no Jew; he was a foreigner, one of those people Peter thought of as "unclean." Now Peter suddenly saw what his vision had meant! If he was no longer to call any kind of animal unclean, he was not to call any kind of man unclean either. So he told the three messengers to come into the house and made them welcome — something he would not have dreamed of doing before! They stayed there overnight and then all set out for Caesarea, and some of the Jewish Christians from Joppa went with them.

When they came near Cornelius's house, he came out to meet them and fell at Peter's feet, as if he were going to worship him. But Peter said, "Stand up. I am only a man, just as you are."

They went into the house talking together, and there Peter found a whole crowd of people waiting for him. Cornelius had called his best friends together to hear what Peter would tell them!

Peter said, "You know that a Jew considers himself unclean if he goes into the house of someone who is not a Jew, but God has been showing me that we should not speak of anyone as unclean. And so, when you sent for me, I came, right away. Tell me, why did you send for me?"

So Cornelius told him all about the angel and his message. "And now you are here," he said. "You see us all ready and waiting to hear what it is the Lord wants us to do."

"I see clearly now," said Peter, "that God does not care what race a man belongs to; He welcomes everyone of any race, so long as he is trying to please Him." With that he started in right away to tell them all about our Lord.

While he was still speaking, the Holy Spirit came down on Cornelius and all his friends, just as He had come down on the Apostles at Pentecost. They began to praise God aloud and to speak in languages they had never learned.

The Jewish Christians who had come with Peter from Joppa, and who had been feeling very doubtful about all this mixing with people who were not Jews, were very much astonished and taken aback.

Peter had told them about his vision, of course, but all the same, they had been wondering if this mixing with people who were not Jews could possibly be right. Well, they had their answer — from the Holy Spirit.

Peter said, "Who will grudge us water to baptize these people, who have received the Holy Spirit just as we did?"

So water was brought, and they were all baptized, and afterward Peter stayed on with them for some days so that he could teach them more about our Lord.

Peter's Escape

Some years after this, Peter had another adventure with an angel in it. Herod, the king of the Jews, was not really a Jew himself and was always trying to make himself liked by the leaders of the Jewish people. So, hearing how annoyed they were by the way our Lord's apostles were spreading His Church, he arrested James, John's brother, and cut off his head. When he found that the

Jewish leaders were delighted with him for doing this, he arrested Peter, too. But by then, it was Paschal time, which he knew was regarded as a bad time for killing people. So he put Peter in prison to wait until the holidays were over. They lasted a week, and all that week Peter was in prison, and the whole Church was praying for him.

Perhaps Herod had heard about the mysterious way the twelve Apostles had gotten out of prison once before, for he was taking no chances with Peter. There were two soldiers in his cell with him, one chained to each of his wrists. And outside the cell door were two more; these four were changed every four hours. There were guards at the prison doors as usual, too. It didn't look as if Peter had much chance of escaping.

At last, the end of Paschal time came, and Peter knew that in the morning he would be brought out of his cell to be killed as James had been. But he slept soundly all the same, and the two soldiers who were chained to him slept, too. Suddenly an angel stood by Peter in the cell, and a bright light shone on the three men sleeping on the ground. The angel struck Peter on his side to wake him up. As soon as he got his eyes open, the angel said, "Quick! Get up!"

Peter began to get to his feet, still very blinky and not at all sure what was happening, and the chains fell off his hands. But the two soldiers still slept.

"Now get dressed," said the angel. "Here, put your shoes on; now your cloak. And now follow me." Peter, still half asleep, followed the angel out of the cell. When he saw that the soldiers standing on guard there took no notice of him or the angel, he thought the whole thing must be a dream or a vision. But he kept on following the angel.

They passed the guards at the prison doors and came at last to the great iron gates that stood between the prison courtyard and the street. Peter watched these gates open for them of their own accord, and he followed the angel through them, and up the street outside the prison. At the end of this street, the angel left him.

And then Peter really woke up and found himself out of prison, free in the dark city streets. "Now I know," he said to himself, "that God really did send His angel to set me free!"

Peter knew a great search would be made for him as soon as it was discovered he was not in the prison. He ought to get out of Jerusalem quietly and quickly. But he had to let his friends know what had happened. For a few minutes he stood and thought what would be the best thing to do. Then he set off for the house belonging to Mark's mother, Mary.

A whole crowd of people were gathered there, spending the night praying for Peter. When he knocked at the door, a girl called Rhoda came to it. She didn't want to let just anybody in, in the middle of the night, so she called out to ask who was there.

"It is Peter," said Peter.

Rhoda was so excited that, instead of opening the door, she went flying back into the room where everyone was praying, calling out that Peter was at the door.

"Nonsense!" they said. "Have you gone mad? How could Peter be here?" But Rhoda kept saying that she knew Peter's voice at once, and it was Peter. "Perhaps it is his guardian angel," someone said, "come to give us news of him."

Meanwhile Peter, who must have wondered why in the world they didn't let him in, kept on knocking at the door. At last, someone thought that the quickest way to end the argument would be to open the door, so they did that, and in walked Peter.

Then there was a great to-do, everyone exclaiming and talking at once! Peter didn't want the whole street to hear that he was free, so he made signs to them to be quiet, and when they were, he told them all that happened. He asked them to let James, the Bishop of Jerusalem, know about it, and all the rest of the Christians. Then he slipped out of the city and was far away before anyone discovered that he was missing from his cell in the prison.

Chapter Thirteen

St. John's Visions

There were once two brothers, one a lot older than the other. The older one, Francis, was in the eighth grade and was to have the best part in the school play. The little one, Jimmy, was too young to go to school at all, but he was determined to see Francis act. His mother was not at all sure it was a good idea. She knew Francis was playing the part of St. Paul and that his head was supposed to be cut off, and she was afraid Jimmy wouldn't like it.

But Jimmy kept saying that he *knew* it was all make-believe, and he *must* see Francis being St. Paul, and in the end he had his way. But alas! When he saw Francis fall down on the stage with tomato-ketchup blood all over him, he forgot about it being make-believe and howled at the top of his voice.

Luckily, St. Paul getting his head cut off was the very end of the play, so Jimmy's mother picked him up and took him straight around to the back of the stage. And, of course, there was Francis, perfectly all right and being praised and congratulated by everybody. Jimmy not only stopped howling; he took the greatest interest in all that was to be seen behind the stage: what the scenery looked like from the back, and the lights, and how the curtain came down, and all the people who were there, helping in one way or another. And then his mother saw that if only she had thought of taking him behind the stage *before* the play, and introducing him to the tomato ketchup that was to suddenly appear on Francis, he would probably have been quite all right.

Now, all of us, whatever age we are, are rather like Jimmy watching his first play! We see what's happening in the world, but we don't see what's happening behind the scenes. Behind the scenes of this world is Heaven. Of course, when a martyr dies for our Lord, the blood he sheds is real, and so is his death. But Heaven is real, too; if we could see behind the scenes, we would see the martyr being praised and congratulated by our Lord and the angels and saints — very much all right and ready to begin the everlasting happiness of Heaven. If we could only see that! If we could only be taken behind the scenes of this world and see the world of spirits it all depends on!

Well, the exciting thing about the last part of the New Testament, which we call the Apocalypse of St. John, or the book of Revelation, is that it is just that: a glimpse behind the scenes. *Apocalypse* means "unveiling," like pulling back a curtain so that you can see what is behind it.

St. John was allowed to see, and was told to tell us, how this world looks from Heaven. He saw God and His angels in charge of all that happens in our world, and he saw something of what is still to happen, especially how it will all end. That is to say, he saw what the happy ending is to be, how God has planned that everything shall work out at last.

St. John couldn't really see God or the angels with his eyes. What he saw was a picture, a vision, and because it was a vision of invisible things, it is full of symbols.

We use symbols all the time and don't even notice we are doing it. When there is a presidential election coming, and often enough when there isn't, we see pictures of an elephant and a donkey in all the papers. Everyone knows that the elephant stands for the Republicans and the donkey stands for the Democrats; they are symbols, and very handy the artists find them. It would be as hard to make a picture of a political party as it would of a spirit.

Many of the symbols St. John uses are easy to understand, but some are not. Suppose you had never heard that an elephant stood for the Republican party and a donkey for the Democrats; how very puzzling those pictures would be! You might guess the artist didn't mean them for real animals, but how would you ever guess what he did mean them for?

Well, a few of St. John's symbols are puzzling for just that reason: when he was shown them, they were quite clear, but in all the long years since, we have forgotten what some of them meant. There are some puzzles in the

Apocalypse for that reason, and some for another reason. It is so full of meaning that it is very hard for anyone to understand quite all of it.

In this book, you will find only a little of it, and not the parts that are hardest to understand.

Why do you suppose God showed it all to St. John? There are all sorts of reasons, but a special one was to stop us from being frightened of the things we see happening in this world. Like Francis's little brother, we have been told there is nothing to be frightened of. We know quite well that God wants us all in Heaven with Him, and that He plans to make us happy there forever and ever. All we have to do to get there is to love our Lord and do as He wants us to; if we do that, everything is certain to be all right. We know all that, but we can't see it, so we get frightened and mixed up and upset over all the wrong things.

So St. John was given this glimpse behind the scenes (just as Jimmy was at the school play) so that he could tell us, "It really is all right. I saw the martyrs who had died for our Lord. They were all there. I saw them given new white clothes to wear. I saw how God prevents even the winds from blowing until we are ready for them; I saw angels holding them back! It is true that some of the things I saw were disasters coming to the earth. I saw War like a rider with a great sword, and I saw Famine with a pair of scales to weigh food with, and I saw Death coming to the earth. But they can come only when God lets them. And I saw what is to happen to the Devil and all his angels at the end of the world, and I saw all the people who will get safely to Heaven at last — such a crowd as no one could count. I promise you, this is a play with a happy ending."

So this last piece of the New Testament is meant to say to us just what angels who bring messages from God almost always begin by saying: "Do not be afraid!"

When John saw these visions, he was on a little island called Patmos. Patmos is in the Aegean Sea, between Greece and the country we now call Turkey. In those days, the part of Turkey nearest to Greece was called Asia. When St. John speaks of "the seven churches in Asia," this is the country he means, not the continent we now call Asia. St. John had been living at Ephesus, a city in Asia, and founding churches all about the country.

St. John was on Patmos because there was a persecution going on, and the Romans who were doing the persecuting wanted to get rid of him. They didn't kill him, perhaps because they were afraid it would make too much trouble, because everybody loved John. Anyway, they put him on this little rocky island, all by himself, instead. John must have thought it a great pity that he should be away from his new Christians, just when they most needed him. But Patmos was where God wanted him, and by himself, so that he would have time to be shown these visions and to write them down. The book he wrote was for the churches in Asia first, but it was for all of us, too — a glimpse of Heaven for the whole Church to learn from.

This is how he begins:

This is a revelation from Jesus Christ, of things which are to happen soon. He sent His angel to show the pattern of it to His servant John. Thus John writes to the seven churches in Asia: Grace and peace be yours from Him who is, and ever was, and is still to come, and from the seven spirits who stand before His throne. And from Jesus Christ, the first of the dead to rise, who rules over all earthly kings. He has proven His love for us by washing us clean from our sins in His blood. He has made us a royal race of priests to serve God, His Father. Glory and power be His through endless ages!

I, John, your brother, who share the same ill treatment as you do, was set down on the island called Patmos, for love of God's word and of the truth about Jesus. There, one Sunday, I fell into a trance. I heard a voice behind me, loud as the call of a trumpet. The voice said, "Write down all you see in a book, and send it to the seven churches in Asia."

So I turned to see who had spoken, and I saw seven golden candlesticks and, in the midst of them, one who seemed like a man.

It was our Lord John saw, but our Lord in the glory of Heaven, not as John remembered Him every day on earth. His face was as bright as the sun at noon, His hair dazzled like snow with the sun on it, His eyes were like flame, and His voice sounded like a river in flood. In His right hand He held seven stars, and from His mouth came a two-edged sword. The sword stands for the word of God, the sharpest of all weapons.

John had seen our Lord in glory once before, at the Transfiguration, but all the same, he was now terrified. He fell on his face and lay, he says, "like a dead man." But as he lay there, he felt our Lord's hand on his shoulder — just as he had at the Transfiguration — and this time, too, he heard the same words: "Do not be afraid." Then our Lord said, "I am before all and at the end of all, and I live! I who died am alive forever. Write down all I show you in a book, and send it to the seven churches in Asia. The seven stars in my hand stand for the angels of the seven churches, and the seven candlesticks stand for the churches themselves."

Then our Lord gave St. John messages to send in a letter to each of the churches, telling them in what they were doing well, and in what not so well. And at the end of each letter, John was to say, "Who wins the victory?" Our Lord tells each church something of what He will do for all those who win their war with the Devil in this world. Here are some of the things He promised them — and promises us, too, if we are faithful to Him:

• I will give him fruit from the Tree of Life which grows in Paradise.

• I will give him a white stone on which is written his new name, which no one knows but the man who receives it.

• I will acknowledge him as my friend before my Father and the angels; I will let him share my throne with me.

This is how John's next vision began: "I saw a door in the sky standing open, and the same voice that I had heard before said to me, 'Come up to my side!' "

So John went up through the door and saw the throne of God and someone on it whom he could not describe at all, except to say that He seemed like a jewel, and that there was a rainbow around His throne "like a vision of emerald."

Around the throne were twenty-four seats, and on them sat twenty-four men whom St. John calls elders. They were grandly dressed in white like kings, and each wore a gold crown. There were seven lamps burning before the throne, and all around it was a sea of crystal-clear glass. Close around the throne stood four winged beings rather like the seraphim and cherubim Isaiah and Ezekiel saw, and they sang a song like theirs, too: "Holy, holy, holy, is the Lord God almighty who ever was, and is, and is still to come." And as they sang, the twenty-four elders threw down their golden crowns before the throne and said, "To You, Lord God, all honor and glory are due; by You all things were made; nothing was ever made but in obedience to Your will." Next St. John writes:

Then I saw that He who sat on the throne had a scroll in His right hand, and it was rolled up tightly and sealed with seven seals.

A great angel cried out in a loud voice, "Who claims the right to open the book and break the seals on it?" But he found no one in Heaven or on earth or anywhere else who could open the book. I was in tears because no one could open it, until one of the elders said to me, "No need to cry! Here is someone who has gained the right to open the book: the Lion of the tribe of Judah; the descendant of David."

Then I saw, in the midst of Heaven, where the throne was, a Lamb standing upright, although it seemed to have been killed in sacrifice. He came and took the scroll from Him who sat on the throne. When they saw this, the twenty-four elders fell down in worship before the Lamb, and they sang a new hymn:

"You, Lord, are worthy to take up the book and break the seals on it; You were slain in sacrifice, and You have ransomed us by shedding Your blood and have given us to God. You have made us a royal race of priests to serve God, and we shall reign as kings over the earth."

Then I heard the voices of crowds and crowds of angels standing about the throne in their thousands and crying aloud, "Power and wisdom and strength, honor and glory and blessing belong by right to Him, and the Lamb who was killed."

And every creature in Heaven and on earth and in the sea I heard cry out together, "Blessing and honor and power and glory forever to Him who sits on the throne and to the Lamb." And the four winged beings like seraphim said, "Amen."

Then, in my vision, I saw the Lamb break open one of the seals, and with that I heard one of the four living beings say in a voice like thunder, "Come and look!"

So I looked and saw a white horse whose rider carried a bow. A crown was given him, and he rode out, victorious and ready to win greater victories.

And when the second seal was broken, I heard the second of the living beings say, "Come and look!"

So I looked. A second horse came out, red as fire, and his rider was given power to take away peace from the earth and set men to killing one another, and a great sword was given him.

When the third seal was broken, I heard the third living being say, "Come and look!"

So I looked and saw a black horse whose rider carried in his hand a pair of scales such as we weigh food with. And I thought I heard a voice say, "A whole silver piece for a quart of wheat, a silver coin for three quarts of barley! Be careful of the oil and wine."

When the fourth seal was broken, I heard the fourth living being say, "Come and look!"

So I looked and saw a pale horse; its rider was death, and Hell went at its bridle rein. He was allowed to have his way with all the world, killing men by the sword and famine and disease and through the wild beasts that roam about the earth.

And when the fifth seal was broken, I saw under the altar the souls of all who had been killed for love of God's word and for the truth they held. They cried out with loud voices, "Sovereign Lord, the holy, the true, how long will it be now until You sit in judgment on those who shed our blood?"

They were each given a white robe and told to rest a little longer until they were joined by the rest of those who were to die as they had died.

Then in my vision I saw the sixth seal broken, and at that there was a great earthquake; the sun grew dark and the moon red as blood. The stars fell out of the sky like unripe fruit from a fig tree when a strong wind blows. The sky folded up like a scroll and disappeared, and the mountains and the islands

155

in the sea were all moved from their places. Kings and noblemen, the rich and the poor, captains and servants, all alike, slaves or free, hid themselves in caves and among the rocks. "Fall on us!" they said to the hills and the rocks, "and hide us from Him who sits on the throne and from the vengeance of the Lamb. Which of us can face Him now that this great day, the day of His vengeance, has come?"

And now I saw four angels standing at the four corners of the world, holding back the four winds, so that they should not blow upon the world and destroy it. And I saw another angel coming up from the sunrise with the seal of the living God. And he cried out to the four angels holding the winds, "Do not destroy land or sea until we have marked the foreheads of those who serve our God."

I heard the count of those who were marked, a hundred forty-four thousand of them, taken from every tribe of the sons of Israel.

And then I saw a great crowd of people, more than anyone could ever count, taken from every nation in the world. All these stood before the throne of God in the Lamb's presence. They were dressed in white, with palm branches in their hands, and they cried out aloud, "To our God who sits on the throne and to the Lamb all saving power belongs." And all the angels who were standing around the throne fell down and worshiped God: "Blessing and glory and wisdom and thanksgiving and honor and power and strength belong to our God forever. Amen."

Then one of the elders turned to me and said, "Do you know who these people are, and where they come from?"

"My Lord," I said, "you can tell me."

"All these," he said, "have come here after great trouble and distress; they have washed their robes white in the blood of the Lamb. And now they stand before God's throne; they always serve Him in His Temple; His presence is all about them. They will never be hungry or thirsty anymore. The Lamb will be their shepherd; He will lead them to springs whose water is life, and God will wipe away the last tears from their eyes."

Then the seventh seal was broken, and there was silence in Heaven for about half an hour.

That is the end of the first part of this vision. The Lamb, of course, is our Lord. His sacrifice on Calvary was the fulfillment of all the sacrifices of the Old Law in which lambs were killed. We still call Him by this name at Mass when we say, "Lamb of God, who takes away the sins of the world, have mercy on us."

The scroll is a book, but not made like our books. In those days, books were written on one very long piece of parchment and then rolled up, and if you didn't want anyone to interfere with it, you tied it up and put your seal on it. What was written on the scroll was the explanation of the whole history of the world, why it was made and why all the things that have happened since then were allowed to happen, and what the end of it all will be. These things are in the hand of God, just as the scroll was. And none of the history of the world makes any sense without our Lord; that's why He was the only one who could break the seals and open the scroll.

No one knows who the rider of the first of the horses John saw was, but he was probably something like the wish to own a great deal of the world that nations sometimes have. The other three are easy: War, Famine, and Death. And none of them, you see, could move unless God allowed them to.

The martyrs who were told to rest a little longer until all the other people who were to die for our Lord came to join them, are waiting still; martyrs are still dying for our Lord today! But if it seems a long time to us, you may be sure it seems only a little time to them; time goes so fast in Heaven.

The silence in Heaven when the seventh seal was broken was, people think, because now everything was made plain, and everyone was lost in wonder. But it seems John was not to tell us about it.

There is a great deal more in John's visions about all the disasters that are to happen before the world comes to an end, but perhaps there are enough disasters told already. So some of the nice things come next, and one of them is an angel that John saw standing by the altar in Heaven. He had a golden censer and was offering incense, and the incense he offered was the prayers of the saints. And John saw a great war in the skies, Michael the Archangel and the good angels fighting against the Devil and his angels. The Devil and his angels were flung out of the sky, down to earth, and there they wander about among us. The Devil is always furious and miserable, and so are all his bad angels, because they have chosen to hate God instead of loving Him. They hate us, too, if we love God, and try to get us to sin so badly that we shall be fit only for Hell, which is their home. God allows them to wander about the world trying to tempt us to sin, because refusing to listen to them helps us on our way to Heaven. At the end of the world, they will be sent home forever, so they are not looking forward to it at all and try to do all the harm they can while they have time.

And now here is a picture John saw of our Lord leading the armies of Heaven, which are the angels, of course — perhaps those twelve legions of angels He would not ask for in Gethsemane:

The sky opened, and I saw a white horse appear. Its rider was called The Faithful, The True. He judges and goes to battle in the cause of right. His eyes were like flame, and He was royally crowned. The name written on His crown is the only one He knows. He wore a garment dyed blood-red, and He is called the Word of God. The armies of Heaven followed Him mounted on white horses and dressed in clean white linen. From His mouth came a two-edged sword, ready to strike the nations of the world. He will herd them, as sheep are herded, with an iron crook. And this is the title that is written on His cloak, where it falls across His thigh: "King of kings and Lord of lords."

And here is a picture of the general judgment, at the end of the world:

And now I saw a great throne, all white, and one sitting on it at whose glance Heaven and earth cowered away. Before this throne, in my vision, I saw that the dead must come, great and little alike. And the account books were opened, and another book, too, was opened, the Book of Life. And the dead were judged by what they had done during their lives, as the books recorded it. The sea gave up those who had been drowned, too, and each man was judged according to his deeds, and Death and the Grave were thrown into Hell. This must happen to everyone whose name is not found in the Book of Life.

And what about the people whose names are found there? Our Lord told us long ago that no one had ever

seen, and no one could guess, what wonderful things
God had prepared for those who love Him. The vision he
gave St. John, just a glimpse of a picture of the beginning
of those things, is wonderful enough to make us long to
see them. The New Jerusalem means the whole city of
God. The first religion God gave the world, the religion
of the Jews, had its headquarters at Jerusalem, and the
Church our Lord founded began from that religion, and
from that city. So the New Jerusalem means the city of all
those who love God, whether they lived before our Lord
came or afterward. And it is called the Bride of Christ because it belongs altogether to Him. This is the vision:

Then I saw a new sky and a new earth. The old sky
and earth and sea had vanished away. And I, John,
saw in my vision that holy city, which is the New
Jerusalem, being sent down by God from the skies,
as beautiful as a bride going to her wedding. I
heard, too, a voice that cried aloud from the throne
of God: "Here is God's house among men; He will
live among them, and they will be His own people,
and He will be with them, their own God. He will
wipe away every tear from their eyes, and there will
be no more death or crying, no more sorrow; those
old things are finished with."

And He who sat on the throne said, "Behold, I
make all things new!" (These words I was told to
write down, words most sure and true.) And He

said to me, "It is over. I am the beginning of all things, and their end. Those who are thirsty shall drink — it is my free gift — from the spring whose water is life. Who wins the victory? He shall have his share in this; I will be his God, and he shall be my son.

"But not the cowards, not those who refuse to believe, not those who lead wicked lives, nor murderers, nor liars, nor those who deal unfairly — all those must go into the everlasting flames."

And now an angel came and spoke to me. "Come," he said, "and I will show you that bride whose bridegroom is the Lamb."

And he carried me off to a high mountain and there showed me the Holy City, Jerusalem, as it came down, sent by God from Heaven, and clothed in the glory of God.

The light that shone over it was bright as any precious stone, and a great wall was raised all around it. There were twelve gates, and twelve angels at the gates, and the names of the twelve tribes of Israel were carved over them.

The city wall, too, had twelve foundation stones, and these were named for the Lamb's twelve Apostles. The walls were made of jasper, but the city itself was all built of gold, but gold that was clear, like glass. And the foundations on which the city was built were made of precious stones; they were of all kinds of colors, green and blue, rose-red and white, crimson, soft yellows and golden-green, violet and blue. The twelve gates of the city were each one single pearl and the streets of pure, transparent gold.

I saw no temple in the city; its temple is the Lord God Almighty and the Lamb. Nor had the city any need of sun or moon to give light; the glory of God shone there, and the Lamb gave it light. The nations will live and move in its radiance; the kings of the earth will bring it their praise and honor.

The gates will never be shut for the night, for there is no night there. They will always stand open, as everyone flocks to it with honor and praise. Nothing that is not clean, nothing that could make anything else the least bit dirty, can ever hope to get into this city; no one can enter it unless his name is written in the Book of Life.

He showed me, too, the river whose waters give life. It flows, clear as crystal, from the throne of the Lamb. On each side of it, along the city streets, grows the Tree of Life and there is fresh ripe fruit on it every month of the year; the leaves of this tree bring health to all the nations of the world.

Never can there be any evil in that city; God's throne — which is the Lamb's throne, too — will be there. His servants will worship Him and see His face; His name will be marked on their foreheads. There will be no need of lamp or sun; the Lord God will shed His light on them, and they will reign forever and ever.

Then the angel said to me, "These words are sure and true. The Lord God who inspires the holy prophets has sent His angel to tell His servants on earth what is soon to happen." All this, I, John, saw and heard, and I fell down at the angel's feet, to worship him. But he said, "Never do that! I am only one of your fellow servants; keep your worship for God."

And finally this command came to John from our Lord:

Do not seal up the words of prophecy in this book; the time is close at hand. Be patient, I am coming soon, and I will repay each man according to the life he has lived.

I am before all, and at the end of all, the beginning of everything, and its end. I, Jesus, have sent my angel to make you certain of this in all your churches. I am the root of all; I am the descendant of David; I am the bright star that brings the day. The Holy Spirit and my bride, the Church, bid me come. Let everyone who hears this read say, "Come."

And we, who very much want to see our Lord come again, the wonderful new beginning of everything that is to follow the end of this old world, say just as He wants us to: "Come, Lord Jesus!"

Biographical Note

Marigold Hunt

(1905-1994)

A speaker for the Catholic Evidence Guild, Marigold Hunt served for many years as advertising manager of Sheed and Ward publishing company.

She had a delightful flair for writing for children, moving her readers with warm, reverent, inspiring words. Her books, which include *St. Patrick's Summer, The First Christians*, and *A Life of Our Lord for Children*, continue to make the Faith come alive for today's children.

Miss Hunt spent her final years in Somerset, Massachusetts, with her friends Patricia and Owen McGowan. She died on December 15, 1994, and is buried in St. Patrick's Cemetery in Somerset.

Sophia Institute Press®

Sophia Institute® is a nonprofit institution that seeks to restore man's knowledge of eternal truth, including man's knowledge of his own nature, his relation to other persons, and his relation to God. Sophia Institute Press® serves this end in numerous ways: it publishes translations of foreign works to make them accessible to English-speaking readers; it brings out-of-print books back into print; and it publishes important new books that fulfill the ideals of Sophia Institute®. These books afford readers a rich source of the enduring wisdom of mankind.

Sophia Institute Press® makes these high-quality books available to the general public by using advanced technology and by soliciting donations to subsidize its publishing costs. Your generosity can help Sophia Institute Press® to provide the public with editions of works containing the enduring wisdom of the ages. Please send your tax-deductible contribution to the address below.

For your free catalog, call:

Toll-free: 1-800-888-9344

Sophia Institute Press®
Box 5284, Manchester, NH 03108
www.sophiainstitute.com

Sophia Institute® is a tax-exempt institution as defined by the Internal Revenue Code, Section 501(c)(3). Tax I.D. 22-2548708.